Unapologetically Black

Doni Glover

Doni Glover
443 858 2684
doni@bmorenews.com
2015

Unapologetically Black

ISBN (978-0-692-40438-6)

Dedication

Dedicated to Asaan and N'yinde Amaari

In Loving Memory of

Doc

Lillie Juanita

Best Friends Marty, Kenny

Table of Contents

Preface

This book is about my life. It started out as a story about my first 12 years in business and my 20 years as a journalist, but turned out to be more autobiographical in nature. I pray that this story, in any event, is a fair depiction of my life, career, and some of the important lessons learned over nearly fifty years of living. Prayerfully, we can reflect on the wisdom of the ancestors as we trek forward as a people and as a human race.

Beyond my story, this book covers my experiences in reporting on the black community's development in my lifetime – beginning in Baltimore and extending globally. I have attempted to provide the best solutions to our challenges as a community. It also speaks directly to black empowerment in the Maryland and Washington, D.C. area. Put simply, I want to see the two million African Americans in this small but significant corner of the world more empowered. We have more black elected officials than ever before. Therefore, I need to see more resources and opportunities going to my people. The return on our investment is dwindling, in my estimation, and I do not like that. Instead of making progress, too many signs suggest that the black community is regressing compared to other groups in America.

For several years, friend and colleague David Miller has encouraged me to join the world's cadre of authors. He has worked with me in the past and is pretty familiar with my personal story as well as my work as a journalist. Having published several books himself, he wanted me to experience the empowerment that comes with being a published author.

Well aware of my love of writing, he consistently insisted that I write and finish this book. I am glad I listened to him.

Kristina Michelle, a woman who has also been very supportive, deserves credit for actually helping me to get started. Having the idea to write a book is one thing; execution is an entirely different story. Hence, I am forever grateful to both David and Kris for the push.

In the process of writing, others were helpful, too. Lutisha Williams is the best prayer warrior and assistant in the world. And Pamela Reaves and Marsha Reeves Jews are both the epitome of a big sister. Meshelle Howard is yet another braveheart whose kind words always inspire me to work even more efficiently and productively. And let's not forget Tion Bolden of Triflava Designs who always delivers quality graphics along with incredible vision.

Dottie Hector, owner of Phillips Funeral Home, has *always* been in my corner. She has known me all of my life and I know that if my parents were alive, they would thank her for all of her kindness and support. As the son of an undertaker, I can honestly say that I am a proud product of the funeral industry – although I chose a different line of work.

Funeral professionals introduced me to the world of business at a young age. The business taught me how to take care of customers. I had the golden opportunity to practice customer service since I was a lad. From answering the business telephone to dealing with bereaved families, I owe so much to the black funeral directors in Baltimore; they put entrepreneurship in my soul.

Further, Dottie Hector is one hell of a businesswoman herself. She is a steady reminder to always be professional, do stellar work, use the best diction possible, and come dressed for the part. She demands that I represent my family and community well whenever the opportunity presents itself – much like my childhood piano teacher, Mr. Barton Bonds.

And, Ms. Dottie urges me to be increasingly political and aware of what is happening in the community. I really appreciate that as black people need and deserve the very best representation possible. And, no one person can be the only watchdog. It takes all of us working together.

I am so very thankful to Lisa, Asaan's mother, and to Nakia Kawan, N'yinde's mother. Because they are exceptional moms, I have never had to worry about my children. Instead, I have been afforded the sacred opportunity to do the work I was called to do. I am very proud of them and pray all the best to them always.

And I grateful for family, friends, and supporters who keep us going: Lois, Desi and Donna Glover; Mr. Hooks; Godmother Marlene Elliott Wilson; Cornell and Sabrina Bass; Everyone's Place Book Store; Time Printers; The Bea Gaddy Center; Kevin Brown; The Barretts; John Wesley; Black Professional Men; James Mosher Baseball; Dr. Tyrone Taborn; Bob Ingram; Scott Phillips; Hassan Giordano; Anthony McCarthy; Choo Smith; Catalina Byrd; CD Witherspoon; WPBNetworks.com and WPBRadio.com's Frank and April Johnson; The Radio One Baltimore Family; Kenny Brown; Malik Rahman; Andy Green; the BaltimoreBrew.com; NewsOne Now with Roland Martin; Jeff Johnson; Kevin Powell; Kam Williams; Wanda Draper of WBAL TV 11; Joy and Peter Bramble of The Baltimore Times; Jake Oliver, Publisher of the Afro American Newspapers; the WEAA 88.9 FM Family; Maryland Public Television's Charles Robinson; Tom Moore of WCBM 680 AM; Armstrong Williams; The US Black Chambers, Inc.'s Ron Busby; Heart and Soul Magazine's Michael Graham; Icetech's William Hopson; Alexis

Coates; The Portland Observer; the National Newspaper Publishers Association and Rev. Ben Chavis; Brother Richard Muhammad, Editor-in-chief of The Final Call; The Land of Kush Vegan Restaurant; Phaze 10 Restaurant; Terra Café Bmore; Robin Smith; Simple Wellness Day Spa; Angela Beard Hardy; Larry Young; Lee Cross; Ericka Alston; Karima Mariama Arthur; Manny Price; S. Curry Trye, Esquire; Russell Neverdon, Esquire; J. Wyndal Gordon, Esquire; Commercial Group; John Bugg State Farm; Bugg & Hardnett; Sanjay Thomas All State; Edible Arrangements *Govans *Randallstown and Setzer Capital Management by Kevin Setzer; the Harbor Bank of Maryland, financiers of my first radio show on WOLB; Sojourner-Douglass College's Dr. Charlie Simmons and Family; Dr. Calvin Burnett; Coppin State University; Morgan State University; Morehouse College; Boonerang Consulting's Jackie Boone; Dewana Daniel of VLRD Management Group; Sean Stinnett; Larry "Pop Pop" Gaines; Izee Auto Body; Sojourner-Douglass College; the Greater Baltimore Urban League; Associated Black Charities of Maryland; Patterson Park Laundry and Dry Cleaners; Sully's Seafood & BBQ; More Hair Salon; Chef JD Ward; Big Bean Theory; Esquire Barber Shop; UMAR Boxing; Renny Bass and the Downtown Cultural Arts Center; Shake & Bake Family Fun Center; Benedetto Haberdashery; Jody Davis Designs; Maurice Dezurn; Monique Smith; NELLA, LLC; Odessa and Rick Hopkins; Sisters4Sisters Network, Inc; Jennifer Hamilton; Micheline Bowman; Lushy Lush; Delegate Dr. Dan Morhaim, M.D.; Dr. Wilbert Wilson; Mayor Eugene Grant; Ervin Bernard Reid; Mark Spencer; Stacy Smith and the Urban Business Center; and Just Juice It at the Avenue Market.

Be audacious. Be black. Be unapologetic.

Unapologetically Black is about a state of being. Donald Glover uses his own perilous journey to draw the reader into his state of being: being black. He tells his story of entrepreneurship and that of being a small business owner, both the immeasurable joy of working for one's self and the not so subtle aspect of being the bill collector, tapping on the window panes of clients with a quarter to make claim on indebted capital in order to continue to operate. Glover is never coy about the mission of his company DMGlobal or its marquee brand bmorenews.com; one of informing black folks of the news. His mission has driven his focus and kept him on pace to expand to both emerging and untapped markets, touching some 200 countries monthly.

I have known Doni some twenty plus years, I have worked in the trenches with him on the campaign trail, he the media expert, I the campaign researcher. I have sat many of times on the other side of the radio booth while Doni has questioned me on a given subject or we debated the issues of the day, always with black folks in mind. For as long as I have known Doni, he has been a one-man operation. He has managed to cover news from the State House to the White House. He is uncanny, unapologetic and uncompromised in his pursuit of justice.

Be blessed. Be prepared. Be influential.

In some capacity or another throughout his entire life, Glover has peddled the news; news that impacts the lives of black folks. I can visualize Doni's early days of selling the Afro Newspaper with satchel and all - hustling. I can see Glover as a business understudy to his dad, soaking up the knowledge of an old-hand, guiding him through the tenants of running a business. It was these lessons that prepared Doni for the call on his life to be a journalist ... a journalist with credentials to cover the White House. I actually remember when I received the call from Doni about receiving his White House credentials. As brothers, we savored in his joy, his fear and the expectation. I was able to do for him what he has done for me and so many others; build him up, encourage him and keep him in reality. Doni has always been the man to help others, share his knowledge and that of others.

Be valuable. Be relevant. Be profitable.

Doni has used the Bmorenews.com platform to shape the image of black people, understanding the power of media, yet bridging the gap between media and black business. This has allowed Doni to cement himself as the Ebony/Jet of Baltimore, utilizing social media and other technology to grow his company into becoming a media conglomerate. While Glover has a vision to do bigger and better things in the future in contrast to the lofty goals of corporate America, Glover emits that of a unique entrepreneurial spirit that touches everyday people. A one-man act, he reaches across political and socio-economic aisles to bring the issues of Black America to the forefront. This book will leave you dusting off the dreams you have shelved for whatever reason - too old, funding, blind wishful thinking, etc. ... and invigorated to do something exceptional.

Be Empowered. Be More.

Marcus Murchison
Political Consultant

Introduction

I am an entrepreneur.
I live, eat and breathe entrepreneurship.
All day. Every day. Even when I'm sleep,
I dream of the next move.
Entrepreneurship. It's a way of life.
Those around me understand this is my mission.
My passion.
Taking absolutely nothing and turning it into an Egyptian pyramid.
Yes. I am determined. I am prepared. I am an entrepreneur. It's in my blood.
From sun up to sun down. I was born for this.
This is what I do.

I am Donald Morton Glover, affectionately known on the airwaves and in local TV news in Greater Baltimore and to a lesser degree, Greater Washington, as Doni Glover. I am an entrepreneur and a journalist, and I am steeped into politics. I live, eat, and breathe business, media and politics all day every day. I was made for this. It is my calling.

Each day my assignment is to tell the story of the African-American experience and be of service to others while earning a decent living in the process. If I can assist some people along this journey, perhaps by helping to get important legislation passed, or improving some existing policies or creating some jobs, then my life will have more meaning. If I can aid some businesses in their growth and expansion, that would be awesome, too.

You see, I realize just as I create opportunities for myself, I must also empower others. Helping others was ingrained in me at an early age. As Luke 12:48 says, to whom much is given much is required. It may be a dying art form, but it's one by which I still live.

I've been so richly blessed and consider it my obligation to give back. Giving back creates beautiful karma – good juju. The ancestors sacrificed for me, so I must also sacrifice for others. And I must help all people, not just black people. My parents called it service, and I've found the more love I give, the more love I get.

As a black journalist with two decades of writing and reporting under my belt, I truly appreciate the magnitude of the black experience, stateside and internationally. I view the black experience across the Diaspora via the political prism and thus my heart goes out to disenfranchised people in societies all over the world, many who look just like me.

As a result of my career, I've become a Pan-African activist, largely through advocacy work for people in Maryland and Washington, which I consider the most political city in the Western hemisphere. I have gotten a lot of joy from being an advocate for black businesses across America and an active proponent of increased trade with Africa and the Caribbean Islands. The thought of blacks collectively doing business throughout the Diaspora simply warms my soul.

I've covered state politics long enough to know how the system can be used to provide educational and recreational resources for youth as well as opportunities for black-owned businesses. I have adamantly joined the push to advance minority business enterprise efforts nationwide, particularly in the Baltimore/D.C. region, and I've loved every minute of it. I've worked at the White House with the relatively new U.S. Black Chambers, Inc., and with the Maryland General Assembly in Annapolis. Even more, we have touched the United Nations in New York City; that's where we held the Bmorenews Global Forum on Women's Empowerment in 2012.

My life as a media entrepreneur is indeed busy. And no two days are the same. All day every day I dream about my next move and ways to better advertise my clients' businesses as well as my own. Thoughts constantly run through my head about how to proceed. My goal is always the same: to expand the footprint of www.bmorenews.com through effective branding. Even when I'm sleep I'm dreaming of my next move. For the brands I manage, I'm continuously striving to devise ways to ensure they're marketed appropriately. I also think about elections and candidates, strategic partnerships, potential joint ventures, who can work together and who cannot, etc.

I put a lot of thought also on planning new Bmorenews.com business networking opportunities embodied in our Black Wall Street SERIES *NYC *MD *DC *ATL and on events catering to our emerging political candidates in different cities and more countries. Yep! Besides my two beautiful children, my life revolves around business, media and politics.

My goal is always to improve the political and economic landscape of my community, beginning in my own backyard. In many ways, I'm also a community watchdog. You wouldn't believe the phone calls I get from people requesting my assistance. It's almost as though I'm an elected official. Apparently, my track record speaks for itself and others recognize that I and my team have become a voice for the voiceless.

Business, media and politics are my mission, and I'm engaged in those realms virtually 24-7. My team aims to help business owners grow their businesses while empowering others through education and inspiration. I absolutely love what I do. Business, media and politics are my way of life and house my state of nirvana. And my goal is always the same: help create a more empowered community that would make the ancestors eternally proud.

Chapter 1
The Beginning

The story begins in 1965 in Baltimore. I was born in the midst of the 1960s revolution, in the middle of the Black Power Movement and at the very epicenter of civic and social change of international proportions. I was born in a city with a rich legacy of empowerment for African-Americans, similar to that bastion of freedom just south of Baltimore in Washington. Black people from this area have a long history of standing tall amidst racial tension and violence.

Historically, such cities offered hope and promise to African-Americans emerging from slavery and had large populations of freed blacks in this dreadful era of American History. In fact, Baltimore had the largest population of free blacks prior to the Civil War. D.C. and Baltimore essentially became hubs and centers of deep black philosophical thought and entrepreneurship. Isaac Myers (1835-1891), the ship builder, is a classic example of the high caliber of black folk who made their marks in Baltimore. Such achievements and the many roles blacks played in untold accounts of American history fuel a peculiar meaningfulness about Baltimore – not just to blacks in this area but to people nationally and internationally. In my opinion, Baltimore is a microcosm of the broader world.

For elite whites, however, just having such a large number of black people eventually always presented a dilemma: what to do with the freed blacks. Baltimore became a national leader in the realm of laws that supported housing segregation going back to the early 1900s. To this day, there are still lines of separation in Baltimore. Sure, it's not as profound, but race is still an ugly factor in my hometown. One way to keep lower-class blacks out of select neighborhoods is by pricing them out; another way is to use the law, such as redistricting.

Even so, when I think of great Marylanders like Frederick Douglass, Harriet Tubman and Thurgood Marshall, I am reminded my birth was no mistake and one of my specific reasons for being is to remind black people of our greatness. For the past 20 years, black achievement has driven my reporting.

African-Americans hail from a proud tradition, despite the negative images often portrayed in mainstream media and a world that hates our blackness and tries to make us ashamed of our beauty. Africa permeates our bones, and to me that means a lot. So I remain encouraged and optimistic and attempt to convince others that despite the obstacles, we're still making progress. We must keep pressing on and trying to better ourselves through the book, the buck and the ballot: that is, through seizing higher education, through mastering our one trillion dollars in annual disposable income, and through our vote. Collectively, I believe they formulate the best strategy for upward mobility in the world. We must remain steadfast and vigilant in our quest to command our rightful places not only in North America but also in the broader global society.

I firmly believe if we tap into our collective greatness as a people we can address our challenges, including providing our youth with jobs. Blacks have a trillion dollars in spending power each year, which means we should be doing a much better job ensuring our young and disenfranchised have ample employment opportunities. Ensuring summer jobs for Washington youth was a staple of Mayor Marion Barry's administration. Barry is a classic example of that fighter spirit that keeps hope alive in Black America. He clearly understood leveraging political power at City Hall into much-needed economic development for the community. Atlanta Mayor Maynard Jackson, the first black mayor of a major southern city, understood economic empowerment for the black community, too. In the building of Hartsfield-Jackson International Airport, for instance, Jackson insisted that black contractors be a significant part of the construction. And when things were not happening fast enough for black contractors, Jackson was willing to cut the water off in order to ensure significant black participation. Barry and Jackson will forever be remembered for their relentless leadership and adamant demands on behalf of blacks. This is the kind of leadership we need today.

As Black Americans to heal, we must look inward and do some serious forgiving. And, we must make sense of the past. It's a tall order to say the least, but it can be done. I'm convinced that love can heal any situation, even the plight of blacks in America. Lord knows we have more than our share of issues, including mass incarceration and a lack of fathers in the home, yet I'm wholeheartedly convinced love can help our situation or any situation.

But back to the story. The 1960s was a time when black people redefined themselves and put their Caucasian brothers and sisters on notice that the days of standing silently by while they dictated how we should look, speak or act were no more. Huge afros and fancy leather jackets were as common among black folk as were family reunions, cabarets and house parties. Man, what a good time to be born! In retrospect, that revolutionary fire for freedom still burns in me today. Blacks everywhere were becoming empowered to demand what a free society should offer every human being regardless of skin color, and my hometown of Baltimore was no different.

Baltimore gave rise to such black people as Tom Smith, who I first learned about from my adopted Godfather, Ed. From 2000 to 2007, Ed owned Paradise, a popular establishment in Sandtown. Over the course of many conversations, Ed and others imparted so much of Baltimore's powerful black history to me. For example, I learned that Tom Smith, who was born in 1871, was the most indomitable black man to walk the streets of Baltimore in the early part of the 20th Century and owned the largest black hotel in the country. Consequently, he wielded incredible influence and money and was one of the richest black men in America and a Democrat with a long track record of philanthropy. Yet despite all of these accolades, few people know about his legacy today.

Tom Smith died in 1938. Since him, other powerful people have emerged from Baltimore, like Thurgood Marshall, Enolia

P. McMillan and members of the Mitchell and Murphy families. And who could forget Mr. Willie Adams, a Baltimore businessman who certainly understood political and economic power? Adams ran a street numbers operation in Baltimore for quite some time, and his wife Victorine Adams was the first black woman on the Baltimore City Council.

In short, there was and is a continuum of black folks who adamantly and vehemently stood up for forward progress over the years. Invariably, there's no wonder I have an unapologetically black mindset. It's truly innate, and anyone who taps into the collective spirit and will of black progress will feel its energy, too.

You see, it's fueled by the blood, sweat and tears of countless African souls who were determined to turn that last sighting of the "Door of No Return" on Goree Island into a positive event in a foreign land, even in shackles. Those ancestors survived so their descendants could live out that spirit of collective power and determination. Certain names rose to stand for the voiceless and speak truth to power to effectuate black empowerment despite all of the ills of American society.

It was the continuum of black political efforts that continually pushed the envelope for black progress. As a result of this power, Judge Harry A. Cole made history in 1954 by becoming the first black person in Maryland to win a State Senate seat. He was also the first black person to serve on the Maryland Court of Appeals. And there were others, like Charles and Joseph Howard, who with others pushed the envelope politically for Black Baltimore beyond the old 4th district to a citywide political platform.

The Howard Brothers were born in Des Moines, Iowa, a town with a history of blacks doing for self and standing up for their rights. They and the Goon Squad, a group of black clergy and leaders, pushed black politics like never before. For example, in 1968 Joseph Howard became the first black person to run for and win a seat on the Supreme Bench in Baltimore.

Mentors of mine like former Baltimore Housing Commissioner Daniel P. Henson, III shared key stories about people such as Milton Allen, Paul Chester, William Murphy, Sr. and Parren J. Mitchell and why 1970 was such an impactful year politically for blacks in Baltimore. According to Henson, there was a "collective will" from the 1960's and 1970's, a mindset of taking power from an unyielding power structure. As Henson often said, "We got to do it for ourselves."

I came on the scene in 1965. Interestingly, one hundred years prior to my birth southern states instituted the *Black Codes* that were designed to incarcerate freed black men. In 1915, fifty years prior to my birth, *Birth of a Nation*, a film that has been a constant reminder of America's ugliest self, was released. The year prior to my birth, Malcolm X founded the Organization of African Unity, the Rev. Dr. Martin Luther King, Jr. won the Nobel Peace Prize and the historic Civil Rights Legislation was passed.

By 1965, America was terribly turbulent. "Black Power! Black Power!" was chanted frequently by people who needed desperately to be heard, recognized and respected, and riots were commonplace in inner-cities. Early that year, Jimmie Lee Jackson was shot to death in Selma by an Alabama state trooper, and Malcolm X was assassinated in February at the Audubon Ballroom in Washington Heights in New York City. March brought the nation "Bloody Sunday" as marchers from Selma to Montgomery, Ala., were attacked on the Edmund Pettus Bridge. The Voting Rights Act of 1965 was signed by President Lyndon Baynes Johnson, and in August of 1965, the Watts Riots literally set South Central Los Angeles on fire.

Hence, on Sunday, June 27, just after noon at Provident Hospital in historic West Baltimore, I was born in the midst of one of this country's most volatile years. Ironically, many of my birth year's events became fodder for this media entrepreneur's autobiography. Indeed, in 1965 the political and social scenes were blazing. Black political activity in Baltimore and in other American cities was hotter than ever and people were justifiably outraged. Black America was a raging bull just beginning to feel its power. At times it was reckless, but it was powerful nonetheless.

Chapter 2
The Birth of Doni Glover

My big sister, Carolyn, nicknamed me "Doni." I love the unique spelling because it reminds me to be myself. I never liked the name Donald, which had no purpose for me. It was my dad's name, but I just don't care for it. Thank God he didn't name me a "Junior". He always said he didn't want me signing any bad checks, a comment I must admit flew right over my head for years.

To be clear, "Donald" was the name my mother called me when I was in trouble or if she needed to get my attention immediately, and it's the name my schoolmates knew me by. It's just that there was a certain formality to it that never quite tapped my fancy. On a brighter note, I eventually learned it means "prince of the universe." Hell, you may wonder who can argue with that important meaning, but when it comes to my name, Doni is my preference.

Besides my sister, I have two brothers, Teddy and Andrei James. They are eighteen, sixteen and fifteen years older than me, respectively, and they've lived in the suburbs for most of their lives. They all are grandparents of some really great offspring. My siblings had a different daddy; their father was my mom's first husband. In any event, my siblings always made me feel loved. So, I'm my dad's only child as well as the baby of the family. And, for the most part, I'm a lifelong urbanite.

I was born to a beautiful woman named Lillie Juanita Glover. Her father, Joaquin Calderon, was a sailor from San Juan, Puerto Rico, and was black. Her mother, Mary, was

African-American and was born in Spartanburg, S.C. I fondly recall those beautiful black and white photos of me lying in a bassinette, which was so indicative of my mom's timeless style, something I fear young girls know nothing about today.

I attended St. Mark's Day Care, Hyman-Blumberg Kindergarten, Matthew Alexander Henson Elementary School #29, William Hugo Lemmel Jr. High School, Baltimore Polytechnic Institute for the 9th and 10th, and finally Paul Laurence Dunbar Community High School. My teachers included Ms. Frances, Dorothy Williams, Frances Parks, Lillian Nottingham, Kermit Williams, Mrs. Hall, and Catherine B. Orange.

Mrs. Hall and Ms. Orange were my two homeroom teachers at Lemmel in the 7th and 8th grade. Let me just state that Lemmel was a serious test of courage. You *had* to fight at that school and there were very few exceptions. I remember seeing security guards get beat up. That's how rowdy the school was, although we had some very exceptional teachers like Ms. Knox, my typing instructor who is still actively engaged in the community. The problem was that the school had students from too many different neighborhoods and clashes consequently occurred on a daily basis. And the girls fought harder than the boys. Through it all, I made the Honor Roll and that made my parents proud; in fact, my prize from my dad was a CB radio. In retrospect, I realize I have been a communications junkie for a long time. Also, I have really come to appreciate how my parents made learning fun and supported my academic pursuits. I know I am fortunate, indeed, because a good education can change everything.

Other incredible teachers I had included my Dunbar instructors like Science Teacher Estella Ingram Levy (who is a friend to this day), Mrs. Woodley, Coach Bob Wade, Uncle Loc (the wrestling coach), and the late Principal, Dr. Elzee Gladden. I must say that the teachers in the Baltimore City Public School system in my time did fine by me and a whole lot of other students who have gone on to do bigger and better things. Their vision and sacrifices in educating me and my peers are priceless. They are a huge reason behind any success here and I will forever thank God for them. Even more, if I ever become governor, I will make sure they have the highest salaries in the nation.

The teachers in my day worked miracles and saved lives as if it were second nature; they did so much more than write-kids up and put them on medication for Attention Deficit Disorder. They recognized problems and they found common sense solutions. People like Mrs. Levy and Ms. Orange can never be replaced in my life. Their love and contributions are what helped me to do my work today and I will always, always, always appreciate their efforts. Shucks! Mr. Williams at Matthew Henson taught me radio at age 10. You know I have madd love for him; he taught us early on about the jazz and R&B legends; he also encouraged us to watch "Roots" when it first came on television. We all did reports on this epic novel about slavery that was the first of its kind. Similarly, I have a lot of love for another educator, although he wasn't my teacher. His name is Brother Charlie Dugger. He is the man who took me on the radio at WEBB and WEAA at the tender age of 15; he also took us to the prisons to do outreach. Even more, he held countless community events that were of a distinctively cultural nature that celebrated black pride. He taught me so much about life and he nurtured hundreds if not thousands of others. Why? Because he loves his people! To say the least, I was blessed with some of the best teachers and mentors in the universe and I know I have to pass on what they gave me so freely.

Our family home was opposite Easterwood Park in West Baltimore, a formerly white neighborhood that was finally integrated around the 1950s. Prior to that, blacks in Baltimore lived closer to downtown in the so-called black areas – around Historic Pennsylvania Avenue on the West and across East Baltimore – where blacks first started. Interestingly, my mom was one of the first black people to integrate this "uptown" Baltimore neighborhood. I so admire and respect her for being determined not only to own her own home but also for living in the neighborhood where she wanted to live – not where someone forced her to live.

Anyway, my mom was very fair-skinned; I figured she could pass for white in her day. Beyond that, she was the greatest woman I've ever known because she had a heart of gold and she was an excellent teacher who loved and nurtured me to no end, while insisting I be the best I can be exactly as a mother should.

"Learn so you can earn!" was one of her favorite sayings. And she had three rules: Number one, "You're leaving my house at 18. You can go to college, join the military or work, but you're leaving here." Number two; "Don't bring any babies in here." Number three, "Own your own home." You see, mom was big on home ownership, perhaps because she had her own home and car as a divorced, single mother of three before she married my father. She ran a tight ship and was quite the disciplinarian. I could go on for days about her, but I will just say that when it came to cooking, she was strictly about her work. Her crab cakes were superb; her Maryland crab soup was unmatchable; nobody could cook stuffed Rockfish like her or pineapple upside down cakes. She also canned fruits and vegetables, including a notorious version of peach preserves. She was simply a beast in the kitchen and put a mountain of love in the food! Heck, her fried chicken was even good cold. That's how well she cooked.

Mom departed this earth in 1985, dying of oral cancer. No question she was a very beautiful woman who died a horribly painful and disfiguring death. At the time of her declining health, I was a sophomore at Morehouse College. Attending "The House" was the most meaningful educational experience I have ever had. I think more than anything, including the fact that Dr. King attended the historic institution - I appreciated the opportunity to imagine doing anything I could possibly conceive. Greatness was all around me at Morehouse, where giants walked. While taking those steps I had a powerful notion of the infinite possibilities in the universe. I guess you could say I was walking on air.

At Morehouse I met people from all over the world, including some cats from Baltimore with whom I became lifelong friends: Leo Hyman (former roommate), Dennis Tillery, Robbie Scott and Adam Scott (no relation). I had completed three semesters at the greatest college in the world for black men, but after mom took ill I landed at Georgia State for a trimester before returning to Baltimore. I was a student at Towson University in the spring of 1985 when my mom passed away. Talk about devastating. My world was turned completely upside down. One minute I was on a cloud, and the next minute I was renting a room because our house got foreclosed, my dad went his way and I went mine. I was only 20. But do know my father was there for me every step of the way. This was merely a reprieve.

In retrospect, I realize I grieved my mom's death unconsciously for years. I was probably depressed at times over her death and didn't even know it. And I was in definite need of therapy. Even though I was the child of a funeral director and had seen hundreds of funerals and had a great understanding of death's impact on families, I can say unequivocally it's totally different when it happens to you. I was just not ready for the loss. I was just not ready to say goodbye to my mother, my girl, my best friend. I just wasn't.

Anyway, I kept it moving and began my own personal college tour, which included Towson University, Johns Hopkins University, Morgan State, the Community College of Baltimore, and lastly, Coppin State. It was at the last three institutions that I actually completed most of the work toward my degree.

Although there were many dark and lonely nights, I am confident it was God's grace and mercy that kept me going at the time. I'm also sure it was the memory of my mom that fueled my desire to succeed. I can still hear my mother's words so plainly, ringing clear and true even today. I can still hear her words of encouragement and remember her acts of kindness, and now I can better appreciate the sacrifices she made for me and the lessons she tried to teach. I can also better understand why she loved me so. In part because of her, I believe I have a special mission to use my gifts and talents to spread love and goodwill while providing empowering information to my people – just like in the early days of the Black Press.

Lillie made only minimum wage at the Methodist Conference Center where she last worked as a receptionist – and a cook on the weekends – but that didn't stop the greatest, most thoughtful care packages a mother could send from arriving at my boarding house. Some of her packages included cash and my favorite item at the time, still-frozen sirloin steaks. Mom sacrificed a lot for me to go to Morehouse, and I will never forget it.

And so, way back in 1985 the seeds for a meaningful media career were being planted. I never realized I was relatively poor until I got to Morehouse and saw cats arriving on campus in Saabs and Benzes – after I walked about 45 minutes just to get there. It didn't matter though, because I had a lot of love in my backpack. Despite my family's financial limitations, my mother never 'faked the funk' and always kept it real. She never pulled punches and kept it honest. So, from that I learned there comes a time when 'it is what it is.' I also learned you have to decide not to accept mediocrity but instead to work harder than the next ten guys and build your castle.

Mom taught me to work with what I've got and to do it to the best of my ability without excuses. And she insisted on doing right by me and supporting me through my flaws to help make me a better man. Looking back, it was her motherly love that nurtured my hunger to do well and make her – and my family – proud. I believe being of service to my family, community, country and world is how I can most appropriately honor her memory.

I will always carry my mom's blood-stained banner in my spirit while continuing to give insatiable love no matter how bleak the odds, how dark the circumstances or how slim the chances. As far as I'm concerned, love is and always will be the answer!

Even though the world can be a mean, crass and insensitive monster at times, I am nonetheless reminded from the very beginning that God *is* and always *will be*. There is nothing you can go through without God being in the midst. We just have to tap into the Holy Spirit.

I never finished at Morehouse. Instead, some thirteen years later and after brief stints at six institutions of higher learning, I landed at Coppin State. Mind you, having grown up four blocks away from Coppin, you could have never told me in a million years I'd go there. It was the college up the street, and going there was totally counter to my mindset. *Surely*, I always thought, *Doni Glover would graduate from somewhere else.*

You see, I never wanted to stay in the neighborhood, not even as a little child. Instead, I always wanted to venture out, expand, explore and search. I'll never forget the day my dad told me travel was the best form of education. When I lived in East Baltimore, I wanted to go to the Westside. When I was west, I wanted to go east.

Before I turned thirteen I'd been to New York, Canada and Florida – quite atypical compared to the travel opportunities afforded most of the kids in my neighborhood.

Despite my humble upbringing, by the time I got to Morehouse I felt right at home. The educational preparation I received at Baltimore Polytechnic Institute from 1979 to 1981 and at Paul Laurence Dunbar Community High School from 1981 to 1983 – incidentally a former national high school basketball champion – well equipped me to stand tall among the best of the best at the nation's premiere black college for men.

Both Poly and Dunbar had some really talented students who have in many cases turned out to be some stellar standouts in this world – from Marty Glaze, Vice President of Commercial Group, one of the most powerful black construction firms in Maryland to former NBA guard Muggsy Bogues, who now runs his own non-profit in North Carolina. I was terribly blessed to go to school with some of the most talented people ever who were unaccustomed to losing at anything. With this spirit inside, I trekked to Atlanta where I learned the definition of hot. I had never experienced such a heat as stifling as Hot-lanta: three showers in one day to stay cool. Coming from Baltimore, it was just unreal.

In any event, I landed at Morehouse with optimism in my eyes, focused on the books and a job – as well as making some meaningful, life-long contacts like upperclassman Robbie Scott from Baltimore, who is still quite the big brother to this day. My college friends later told me I actually stood out in the crowd, which at the time was totally unbeknownst to me. As a freshman, I served as Poet Laureate at Morehouse. It was a serious responsibility, but I was just doing what I'd always done: applying myself. That year I spent most every Sunday afternoon sharing an original poem at Vesper Hour in the MLK Chapel. Not bad for a kid from Baltimore. That experience was a reminder that anything is possible if we just assert ourselves.

While writing this book, I was reminded of the exceptionally well-rounded experiences I had growing up that led to even greater opportunities down the road. In contrast, I guess I thought my experiences were the norm, but in retrospect I realize a lot of my childhood friends did not have the same experiences for whatever reason or reasons. Truth be told, I have never been accustomed to limitations. Today, I better appreciate the various morals and skills I've learned throughout my life, like honesty, integrity and using a computer. I so appreciate the exposure and access my parents provided for me, and I hope my children, in turn, will be able to do the same should they become parents.

For example, I have the distinct pleasure of having come through James Mosher Little League, the oldest black continually operating little league in the country. Former Baltimore Mayor Kurt L. Schmoke and Congressman Elijah Cummings played in the league, along with several hundred others. As a matter of fact, I have the distinct pleasure of being a proud member of The Mets, the 1976 James Mosher Little League Champions. In all, 20,000 to 22,000 young boys have come through that league over 55 years. Even more, I have been asked several times to emcee the Opening Day Ceremony in April, something I treasure dearly. I also got the opportunity to emcee the league's 50th Anniversary. It just doesn't get any better than that.

Another great experience I had was attending the Druid Hill Avenue YMCA, home of the Phalanx Fraternity of which my dad was a member. It is the fifth oldest black YMCA in the country and the oldest branch in Maryland. There I made a lot of friends in West Baltimore. We still lived on the Eastside at the time, but my parents insisted I be connected to some of the city's critical institutions nonetheless. I was probably the only Eastsider at the Druid Hill Y, but it was worth every minute. I got to swim, box and to use the sauna, to play pool, ping pong and bumper pool, to learn karate, go camping and to lift weights. Trust me. Those were the days for real!

When it came to church, my dad was very serious; those early teachings and time in the house of the Lord surely made a difference in my life. I spent my formative years at Perkins Square Baptist Church at 2500 Edmonson Avenue, where I participated in everything from Boy Scouts to Vacation Bible

School to reading and reciting scriptures to playing the piano for Sunday School one Sunday a month. I got paid ten bucks to play. In short, my dad and I attended every Sunday; further, he was also the church treasurer.

Every week I'd watch as he and the co-treasurer, Mr. Al, counted the money. When dad took the money to the bank on Monday morning he was always strapped, something that truly fascinated me. Even more, I admired the fact that *my* dad had earned the trust of the church. What a privilege *and* a responsibility!

Several members from both sides of my family belonged to the church, including Aunt Idella and Aunt Edith, so it was like a home away from home. On Sundays except Communion Sunday, Mrs. Inez Lucas and her team made and sold hot rolls by the dozens, and people came in from all over town for them. It was a great example of community outreach, if you ask me. "Hot with butter and jelly! I'll take a half dozen to start, please." I can still close my eyes and hear people from all over town ordering them. I also vividly remember one Sunday morning at church when I looked around and pondered the very meaning of life. I couldn't have been more than nine or ten. I peered at the beautiful couple who always sat on the other side of the aisle from my dad and me and wondered just how their life was because they were always immaculate and never missed a Sunday. I never found out the answers to the questions I had about them, but I ultimately found the answer to why any couple would be in church together every Sunday. Without God and faith, people are often lost. I have come to appreciate those with a strict regimen when it comes to their faith, whatever that may be. I say, be hot or be cold, but being lukewarm is unforgivable! I just take faith seriously. I have come to know that keeping God first in all I do is unquestionably the best thing I can do in any and every situation.

The way I see it, that couple and everybody else ought to be in church, a mosque or some place of worship on a regular basis. Why? For the food, of course. Not a physical meal, but for a healthy spiritual serving. I'm confident God is real and on time. He may not come when you want him, but He's always right on time.

He's the same God that brought me through my dark times that included abuse of crack cocaine, heroin, powder cocaine and liquor, a couple of reckless relationships, a number of after-hours and after after-hour spots and a multitude of other bad situations that easily could have cost me my life or my freedom. I was headed to damnation, mostly because I was wasting God's blessings. I had lost my way, indeed. Yet in my darkest hour I called on God in the name of Jesus, words I hadn't said since I was a young child. I had wrestled with Islam, Christianity and Judaism for years. Who was right? Who was wrong? I'm here and unabashed to say when it was the absolute ugliest, I called on the name of Jesus, and I'm so very glad I did.

God, I'm convinced, looks beyond our faults no matter how egregious our behavior and sees our needs if we reach out to Him. *Thank you, Lord!* I've found that our job is to learn life's lessons and eliminate unbecoming habits. I've learned if I'm truly sorry, I won't have to say it. My actions will speak for me. People know when you're doing right and they know when you're doing wrong. So, day by day, I'm learning to walk in the light.

My pops was an undertaker, which puts me in a unique clique of people. You've heard of a PK, or preacher's kid. Well, I'm a UK, or undertaker's kid. It's an elite group of individuals who share a common bond that peers beyond this side to the next. Rarely discussed or talked about, ours is a unique family and brotherhood, one entrusted with 'the final ceremony'. We have watched our parents repeatedly and collectively take care of thousands of bereaved families in Baltimore, known by some as "Bodymore." Baltimore has gained a reputation over the years because of its notorious murder rate.

Truth be told, I was nine before I lived in a regular house. Before age nine, I lived on the Eastside above a double-house, where the first floor housed my daddy's funeral chapel. Let's just say by the time I was five, I'd seen more dead bodies than most people see in a lifetime. My dad taught me not to be afraid of the dead. He always said that "It ain't the dead ones who can hurt you. It's them live ones you gotta watch!"

But rest assured his words didn't stop me from haul-tailing out of the embalming room in Frederick, Maryland, when the supposedly dead man on the slab sat straight up. Gas sometimes causes a body to have a final bowel movement. I had to be about five, and it scared the shit out of me! All I know is I went a 'running like Jesse Owens, and nobody was going to stop me! Earl Campbell couldn't have run harder. I saw my father laughing out of the corner of my eye and heard him say, 'Come back! It's okay!' but I never looked back.

My father was Donald Edward Glover, also known as "Doc" Glover. His father was Sam Glover and his mother was Flossie. Sam died at forty-four from diabetes, so John Rivers became the only grandfather I had. I spent a lot of time with Grandma Flossie and Grandpop after school until my dad picked me up and we headed back to East Baltimore. Granny lived at 2100 Westwood Avenue, just up the street from my school. I never met Sam or my mom's father, Joaquin. Sam Glover's dad was from Orangeburg, S.C. Flossie's mother was Mollie Morton, a woman part black and part Indian. My father always said she was Blackfoot; I later learned that she was probably of another tribe. She lived in South Boston, Virginia. If you knew my father you'd know he told me many, many stories about everything from life on Tobacco Road to life in the Korean War. The man was a genius. And let's not forget my mother was pretty dang smart herself to be one of the first black homeowners in a white neighborhood.

A proud and accomplished funeral director and mortician, my father was the most incredible man I have ever met, and he was certainly the wisest. Though one of his greatest personal honors was serving a term as President of the Funeral Directors and Morticians Association of Maryland, he shaped me to be a journalist from the ground up. He would have loved for me to be a funeral director and carry on the family business, but he taught me as a young child to read and to carefully watch the news. The news media bug hit me early on. It's almost as though dad knew it was my calling.

My mother taught me how to love. My dad showed me how to handle the world and also how to fight. He never gave up on me and insisted I could beat crack cocaine. He showed me the world I would one day inspire, but sadly, he passed away suddenly in 2003.

I can recall race being a constant topic throughout my household all my life. My earliest childhood memories include the riots of the 1960s. I can recall National Guardsmen standing guard on my daddy's business' front on Patterson Park and Lanvale in the heart of East Baltimore when I was three. I can recall sneaking the word "niggie" out my mouth at age five with the understanding that it was a bad word that was derogatory to black people and that I shouldn't be using it.

I can recall at night how black people were acting out, looting, burning property and stealing goods. I recall when the Suburban Soda Company down the street put glass on top of their cement walls to keep out looters. I remember seeing burning steel wool fly through the air, obviously an expression of the rage and disdain felt by black folks as the nation mourned the assassination of Rev. Dr. Martin Luther King, Jr. on April 4, 1968.

Although I had no clue as to what was happening to our nation, I sensed turmoil. And I also sensed the sleeping giant was awakening. I was only three, but even then I could see people were out of control, mad and hurt. They were tired of being treated unfairly and were uniting toward a common enemy.

Add in the many families disaffected by Vietnam, and all one can conclude is that America was on the verge of collapse. The powers-that-be were clearly intent on putting black unrest to sleep, or placating the people.

Somewhere around this time, heroin flooded the black community in Baltimore, New York and other "Chocolate cities."

These early memories of my life were in East Baltimore, known for its historically high murder rate and also for its strength. In fact, that's where I began to demonstrate an explorer mentality. Take, for instance, the evening I decided to walk to West Baltimore. I was about six or seven and got about four blocks from home before getting lost. The Good Humor truck man saw me, recognized immediately that I was lost and took me home. Of course my mother whipped my ass. Then she hugged me, told me not to do that again and said I scared the shit out of her. She also told me she loved me more than anything and in that moment let me know my actions, though not intended to cause harm, can deeply hurt others.

In retrospect, she must have been going crazy not knowing where I was. Now that I think about it, I had a flair for travel early on. So, considering my global focus today, I can honestly say it has always been part of my personality to want to go and explore.

East Baltimore, as depicted in part by HBO's *'The Wire'*, has a reputation for a lot of shootings, drugs and prisons. On the positive side, it also has a reputation for some of the world's greatest athletes and noted figures, including Dunbar High School basketball standout Skip Wise, Baltimore's first black Mayor, Clarence "Du" Burns and TLC Beatrice's Reginald F. Lewis, the former captain of the Dunbar Poets football team who shook up the business world with his historic corporate takeover.

My early days in East Baltimore taught me survival and the importance of standing up for yourself. I lived on the Eastside until 1972 or so and learned that people will take advantage of you if you let them. I also learned the failure to stand up for yourself could result in death.

In 2011 during the Baltimore citywide election campaign for mayor and city council, I did a video expose on my childhood neighborhoods – North Avenue and Patterson Park and North Avenue and Greenmount. I found that these neighborhoods – despite the millions of dollars that had come through Baltimore via non-profit and federal funds – had not been touched, rehabbed or renovated in my nearly 50 years. Sure, the area surrounding Johns Hopkins Hospital, the titan, has been redeveloped, but not the rest of the community and this bothers me deeply.

The irony is that other parts of the city get attention all of the time. Why don't black neighborhoods get the same love and attention as do white neighborhoods in Fells Point and Bolton Hill? I'll tell you. The simple, sad and true answer is they're home to poor black people who are often non-voters, and they don't matter to the powers-that-be. This is pathetic and bothersome. In a city where black folks once had significant cohesiveness and power, we're not running much of anything today. It's a serious step backward to say the least.

Interestingly, this same East Baltimore community is home to one of the greatest research institutions in the world, Johns Hopkins. I should add that during the first and second Obama elections, black voter turnout was remarkable in Baltimore, even in the most economically challenged neighborhoods. This is so telling, so beautiful, and so inspiring – although one of my political pundit colleagues, Marcus Murchison, insists it was an anomaly. We agree to disagree on that topic.

East Baltimore is also where, at an early age, my father taught me how to catch a bus across town to the Westside to attend Matthew Henson Elementary School. The number thirteen bus was my first 'passport' to travel. I'd catch the bus from North and Greenmount to West Baltimore at the intersection of North and Pulaski. That was quite a distance for an eight-year old. Thank God I managed. People can't let their children do that today, unfortunately, because it's far too dangerous nowadays.

Another thing: when neighborhood kids from 20th Street would tease me about my dad's work, "Black Stevie" and I would lock them in my father's morgue until they screamed. We got a big kick out of that. "Black", aka Stephen Davis, is another lifelong friend I still have the pleasure of knowing. As a matter of fact, he and my dad share the same birthday.

Eventually an opportunity came for my dad to succeed Mr. Charles R. Laws at a more modern West Baltimore funeral home just outside of downtown. To his credit, each funeral home dad moved to was progressively more sophisticated than the one before.

As for living arrangements, we moved back to my family's Westside home on Moreland Avenue, and I have since been a member of that community. I'm one of those Baltimoreans who boldly loves the East and West of town equally.

Even more, I can tell how drugs and violence have ripped up so much of the black community in both parts of town. Suddenly, the Black Power movement was being replaced by a heavy drug culture and black folks were catching hell. Mass incarceration would go from 300,000 back then to 2.3 million today, too many of whom are black and male.

Once we moved to the 1500 block of Moreland Avenue, the greatest block in the world, a whole new world opened up to me. I was about nine. My oldest best friend, Marty Williams, and I shared a lot of great memories, including our first summer jobs. Our families had known each other for a generation. Marty passed suddenly a couple years ago, and so I have come to treasure those Moreland Avenue memories even more. Moopy and Ed were my other compadres on the block. While I started off having to fight the two brothers all the time in order to gain respect, the two remain close still today. What makes this dead end block so great, of course, is the full access to the ever glorious Senator Troy Brailey-Easterwood Park. The park is roughly two-square blocks with a recreation center, tennis court, basketball court, baseball field, football field and a softball field. To say the least, there are a lot of fond memories. There are also a lot of folks from that neighborhood who didn't make it, like L'il Reggie and Darryl Motley; they died before touching adulthood.

I know it is by the grace and mercy of God that I live today. Surely, I could be gone. I saw death more than a couple times. I saw people get shot and killed. I saw a man shot to death on Baker Street; the blood pouring out of his head onto the street was so thick, so red. I've also come to recognize and appreciate just how blessed I was to have my mother *and* father in the house and the supernatural difference it's made in my life. Many of my peers in the neighborhood did not have both parents around, let alone parents who were entrepreneurs. I was so very fortunate and may have been a tad spoiled, but I have since come to definitely appreciate the wise lessons from the elders. Today, I appreciate anything and everything someone might do for me, however small. If you give me a glass of water, I'm going to thank you like you hit the lottery. Why? Because nobody owes you anything; so, be grateful. Grateful is my word, all day every day.

Now, outside of our sacred block on Moreland Avenue was a jungle. Around the corner on Warwick Avenue, for instance, a lot of cocaine and heroin were sold on a regular. Truth is, nobody told us we were living in the middle of a war zone that featured drugs. Truth is, my part of town was probably considered 'collateral damage' and high casualties were the expected norm. We just didn't know it; we were kids. I believe my neighborhood had as many if not more 'king pins' per square block than any other neighborhood in town – especially when crack took off in the 80s and early 90s. I remember things getting wild and crazy during the Ronald Reagan era. Today, Coppin State now owns much of that old turf and the remaining neighbors have a reprieve from the associated killings and overdoses that come with illicit drugs. I should add that while we had a strong criminal element in our neighborhood, our block on Moreland Avenue also produced some of the most accomplished individuals in the city, like Jean Williams and Mike Cryor. Yep! My community produced some of the best in the world on both sides of the law. You can either keep the words "Chapter One" above, or replace them with a chapter title, or use both. Whichever way you prefer.

Chapter 3
Unconditional Love

Needless to say, as the child of an undertaker I experienced an upbringing that was a tad different than most. "Doc" Glover was a visionary and considered among the best in his craft nationally. He was a proud member of both the local and the national Funeral Directors and Morticians associations, and he wouldn't miss a convention if his life depended on it.

On top of that, he had a great sense of humor. I can recall his insisting on taking me to the front door of my junior high school once in the hearse. I tried to get out at the corner, but he was not having that.

Words cannot express how proud he was to be a funeral director, a businessman and an entrepreneur. He loved his profession with every fiber of his being. During his presidency he was about progress and education, emphasizing new technology and the need to adapt. He was also one hell of a mentor and made it his business to invest in younger professionals like my Dunbar High School schoolmate, Derrick Jones, who has been a funeral director and mortician since he graduated in 1982.

To my dad, the opportunity to head the Funeral Directors and Morticians Association of Maryland was like becoming president of the United States. He was so very proud and focused on improving the quality of the industry in all member funeral homes, and I'm glad to know he got his chance to be president because I'm pretty sure it meant the world to him.

As his son, I learned the Funeral Directors and Morticians Association of Maryland is among the oldest groups of black undertaker associations in the country. It was founded in 1904, the same year as the Great Baltimore Fire. Specifically for black funeral directors, it's actually older than the national association. In other words, black funeral directors in Baltimore have been large, and in charge for a long time, and their role in the lives of many families in Baltimore are simply irreplaceable.

Over the years my father filled my brain with a ton of information about the funeral industry, Baltimore history, and the many families he served. He even told me about the final honors for some really beautiful and accomplished people.

While having a funeral home director for a dad had a stigma attached, I came to embrace it while taking immense pride in what my father did for the community. Countless times he performed his duty, even when the decedent's family's money was short. As a matter of fact, one of my tasks in the family business was collections. I'll never forget my dad telling me to use a quarter when rapping on the window pane. You see, when people don't have your money, they tend to duck you. This tactic is a counter-move designed to get them to the door most expeditiously. It's worked many times and sounds very authoritative.

Whatever you did, you didn't want to owe my father any money. Damn if he wouldn't knock on your window with a coin when you least expected it. He taught me that this was the most annoying sound, obnoxious even – but effective. More than that, he taught me how to collect money, about human behavior and the concept of counter strategies.

He was also excellent at marketing. Business cards, ink pens, calendars, magnets and church fans -- you name it, and he marketed just about everything an undertaker would. Having learned from the giants in the Baltimore industry decades prior, he was a national visionary in the funeral industry.

My father was also a character and had a way with words. Although he was a little rough around the edges at times, he was really mushy inside with a heart of gold. That had to be what my mom saw in him because she, too, had a heart of gold.

He helped a lot of people, served a lot of families, and assisted countless churches, social, Masonic and fraternal organizations. He understood the principle of giving back. And he insisted I learn it as well.

You weren't blessed until you tasted my mother's macaroni and cheese. I've tasted a lot of mac and cheese from all over including dishes prepared with lobster, and yet nobody out-cooked Lillie Juanita Glover! Why? She put a lot of love in her cooking, but you'd have to taste it to fully understand what I mean. Her food danced on my tongue for twenty years, to say the least.

On that note, I'll never forget the time my mother gave me two plates wrapped in aluminum foil. I had just finished dining on her incredibly delightful Thanksgiving dinner with her oyster dressing that just made my heart sing. And her cakes ...

Pineapple Upside Down and German Chocolate were my favorites.

Anyway, she told me to take the two plates and give them to somebody. I asked, "Who, Ma?" She replied, "I don't care. Anybody!"

I turned and looked at her, and she was dead serious. My mother taught me right then and there the meaning of unconditional love – the meaning of life. Who to give it to? She said, "Anybody. After all, everybody's gotta eat." She also used to leave money for the trash men on Christmas. In retrospect, that was a time when people were not as callous as we've become today. We in the black community are as bad off as it gets in many ways nowadays. May the lyrics in Marvin Gaye's hit "What's Going On" again touch our hearts so we can revert to truly caring for one another.

Years later, I met the late Bea Gaddy, the Mother Theresa of Baltimore herself. Let me tell you -- it was one of the greatest memories of my life. My mother was long gone by then. However, Bea Gaddy was nothing short of the lesson my mother had taught me years prior: Unconditional love, especially for the less fortunate.

Bea Gaddy, according to Baltimore's greatest living photographer J.D. Howard, could go into an alley, a hole or wherever the homeless were in Baltimore and call out some names and one by one homeless people would come out of nowhere.

"Johnny, Billy, Mike! I got some hot soup and some blankets! Come on out and get warmed up!" ... or something like that.

Bea Gaddy was a patron saint who loved people and had a soft spot in her heart for the homeless, likely because she and her children were once homeless. See, she understood their plight firsthand. Despite her humble background, Gaddy was elected to the Baltimore City Council.

As I recall, she wasn't very popular among her City Council colleagues. If you ask me, many of them were jealous of her because she came from 'the bottom' so to speak, and because the people so adored her. The lesson here is that it doesn't matter where you start; it's where you finish. The possibly envious Council members felt like, at least in my opinion, they were more deserving of the position than she.

Mind you, she won her seat without going the traditional route and without a political organization behind her – much less the powerful Eastside Democratic Organization (EDO). Everybody came through EDO, so who was Bea to forego it? After all, the EDO was founded by Clarence "Du" Burns, Baltimore's first black mayor. "Du" Burns inherited the seat from William Donald Schaefer after Schaefer became Maryland's governor.

Bottom line, Gaddy, like my mom, understood people and their proclivities and decided to use her life to be a blessing to others, mimicking my favorite American shero, Harriet Tubman. And like another favorite, Malcolm X, Gaddy was intent on accomplishing her mission of feeding and clothing homeless people. Given the spirit of life in our souls, I know that even in our darkest hour God will be revealed to those who are diligently paying attention and will provide refuge in our time of need.

Bea Gaddy gave the shirt off her back and even her own bed to people in need. She was humble enough to receive God's grace, and she warranted the admiration of countless people. Her love, passion and commitment for making the world a better place was evident, even to a little child. Even today, Bea Gaddy's Annual Thanksgiving Day Dinner continues serving and bringing honor to her name. In 2011, it fed 50,000 blacks, whites and a burgeoning number of Latinos.

Another person I think exemplifies unconditional love is Diane Bell-McKoy, the former President and CEO of Baltimore's $100 million federally funded Empowerment Zone. I adopted her as my mom several years back, and she adopted me as her son. I have never met a person who loves her people like she does. Even more, she knows how to organize, meet deadlines and successfully manage $100 million. I can't speak for you, but where I come from that's huge! She loved Marion Barry, served under Kurt L. Schmoke's administration, is one of my living sheroes and is just simply amazing. She, too, has a heart of gold. And she also understands power brokering, which simply tantalizes my mind.

My father, though he was stern, demonstrated agape love, and I've come to truly appreciate that about him. For instance, he gave neighborhood kids who were going to college a piece of money as an incentive to not only go but to do well. I strive to give love and money wisely and to keep love at the center of every single thing I do. Today I strive to make a difference with what God has given me, for I have truly been blessed more than most and don't for one second take that for granted. Doing so, I think, would be like slapping God in the face.

I've come to understand that life is God's gift to us, and what we do with it is our gift back to Him. Therefore, I have a huge responsibility on my shoulders. I've been 'better than blessed' in contrast to most people across the world. That's why I toil arduously to give back. This is the key lesson for us all, best put by my late dad: "With a closed hand, nothing gets in and nothing gets out. However, with an open hand, there are endless possibilities." The moral to the story is to help somebody. Another critical lesson so many never learn is to give selflessly of self to be of service to others.

Every great man and great leader understands service is the pathway to heaven. Likewise, it is in giving that we receive and in serving that we are served. It is in blessing others that we are blessed. These are my values. Now I'm no saint, and I'm not perfect. But with these ideals firmly planted in my heart, I set out to become a strong force in the world of independent media, with my best attempt rooted in unconditional love! My goal has always been to best portray the turbulent struggle and journey of a beautiful, yet resilient race of people who were taken from Africa.

How would I do this? In the process of repairing my life after a decade of decadence, I absolutely had to finish what I started at Morehouse.

I had endured my mother's passing and survived a lifestyle of mindless and reckless behavior and now knew it was time to do something meaningful with my life. The only question became at what school. If I'd had the money, I would have gone back to Morehouse because I am *still* in love with the greatest institution in the world. But, Morehouse was out of the budget, and I needed to make a decision. Ten years after my illustrious college career began at Morehouse; Doc Glover honored my request to help me to return to college. Once I had my dad's support, he said he'd pay for me to go to Coppin. And he had to pay only for the first semester because in the spring of 1994 I was given a full honors scholarship in the Ronald E. McNair Post-Baccalaureate Achievement Program thanks to my nearly 3.5 GPA.

Chapter 4
From Sandtown to Citywide

I have always believed there is a special blessing for the entrepreneur, particularly the African-American entrepreneur. And I have always believed God helps those who help themselves. Hence, drop me in a jungle buck naked without anything, and I'm going to emerge with an outfit and a meal, a big screen TV and a DVD player. That's just my mindset.

I come from parents who were full-time entrepreneurs for much of my childhood, so I inherited my 'hustler' mentality. I'm always open to money-making opportunities because that's all I've ever known. I've had about 50 different jobs ranging from stock broker trainee at The Chapman Company to telemarketer at Citicorp to a long line of hospitality industry positions. At hotels I've worked the front desk, been a bell hop, busboy, head waiter and maître d'.

As a young waiter I began finding my own place in the universe and came to better see how I could successfully pull things together for the sake of business – albeit in a restaurant. By then my creativity was coming together nicely. In this industry I learned to make a boatload of money by selling food and drinks, including stuffed lobster tails, crab cake and shots of Louis XIIIth for seventy-five dollars a pop at Harrison's Pier 5 Restaurant. Chuck Harrison, when we first met, promised I'd make more money working for him than I'd ever made before. He was right.

You see, since my days selling *Afro* newspapers on the MTA buses, I've been bitten with a lasting desire to make more and more legitimate money. No doubt my parents had everything to do with my entrepreneurial grind. Understanding and mastering business and sales became a consistent part of my journey. The restaurant world provided my first taste of good, honest money and opened my mind to more possibilities.

In 1992 I enjoyed being part of the original crew of the brand new $23 million Harrison's Restaurant and Hotel, an establishment on the Inner Harbor. I'd had a similar experience when another new hotel opened on the harbor in 1989. By now I realized I'm attracted to the best of things and the newest of things. I also love originality and have come to appreciate all that it takes to make a business grow and remain profitable. A huge lesson I can impart is always take care of the customer and remember the adage, "The customer is always right." Now please understand that in saying that I'm not implying a customer has the right to abuse his or her server. I'm not saying that by any stretch because that's not the case. Likewise, I know some customers are quite challenging, but you should always strive to satisfy customers.

As a waiter, I tried to earn top sales honors every month, and great management afforded me the opportunity to outsell most anyone who stepped on the restaurant floor. I will add that two other waiters gave me a good run for the money: George, a white guy, and Tony, a black guy from out West. Every day I was sharp, well groomed, polite and funny – and often outsold everybody. Getting customers to order stuffed lobster tails and Louis the XIIIth seemed to be my forte, especially to the big rollers who came in their yachts. But that was back then, in the early 1990s.

Coppin and the Sandtown-Winchester ViewPoint

By 1993, I 'd shaken the fast money bug enough to return my focus to finishing college, this time at Coppin State. You couldn't have told me in a million years I'd be attending college up the street from my childhood home. After all, I'm very much the adventurer and love traveling. A lesson here: Never say never! A second lesson: Be grateful for any and all blessings, however small. And a third lesson: You can say where you have been, but you can't say where you're going. As a matter of fact, my dad used to say that all the time!

I'll never forget the day a restaurant co-worker named Amber politely reminded me that being a waiter was not her top goal in life and she was waiting tables merely to make money to finish her undergraduate degree. Similarly, I hadn't become a waiter to do it for the rest of my life as I, too, aspired to finish college. Besides, I wanted my weekends and holidays back. I wanted to be normal again. I had learned fast money has its trappings and anything worth having is worth working for. While I became pretty good at waiting tables the restaurant business brought out the beast in me. I was money hungry. My sole focus was money. And now that I was back in school, my journalism career was solidified.

And so, in 1993, I returned to college. In 1994 I became co-editor of the *Sandtown-Winchester ViewPoint* after volunteering briefly in that capacity. I graduated three years later with Honors. It was at Coppin that I honed one of my passions and part of my purpose in life because my major, English: Media Arts and Broadcast Technology, is what led me to edit the *Sandtown-Winchester ViewPoint*. Well, in truth I have to attribute the Sandtown gig to my spoken word. You see, I once had the audacity to share a poem in public and community advocate Jerry Cross heard me and became my saving grace. He, Norman Yancey and others shared that "Sandtown" love with me and helped remind me of my mission. To this day, those cats remind me to love myself. They say you can't love anybody else if you don't first love yourself. Day by day I work to be a better person. As they say, if you don't know, you'd better ask somebody. Really and truly, I thank God for them.

Each month, we published about 6,000 copies of the Sandtown community newspaper, typically a 48-page tabloid, and distributed it throughout our 72-square block Historic West Baltimore community. I went from co-editor to editor and eventually to managing editor. I was so very blessed to find my calling, and once I did I began working day and night on news. I lived it, ate it and breathed it.

News was my newfound passion! My job was to fill the newspaper each month with good news and information that was indicative of the positive changes happening in my community thanks to a lot of federal, state and city dollars.

Bill Clinton was president at this time, and a lot of money was being funneled through my community for transformation.

Money was going into new buildings and programs, some specifically for high school drop-outs.

After graduating from Coppin with honors, in 1996 I went to Morgan State University to complete the course requirements for a master's in international affairs. I am a thesis shy of completing that degree.

<u>Going to Work at Baltimore's Empowerment Zone</u>

In 1999, I was hired as a public information specialist at the Baltimore Empowerment Zone, while, mind you, I was still writing for the community newspaper. I was also beginning to test the waters with my own media outlet, *SandtownLive.com*. I knew there was money to be made if I had the right media outlet, namely a vehicle that I controlled.

As I sold ads for the Sandtown newspaper, I realized what potential value it had and that the media is a viable industry. I actually believed I could do for myself what I was doing for Sandtown and had the audacity to believe I could create my own media outlet and sell enough advertising to feed myself and my family. The groundwork was in place for my next logical step to run my own shop. Thus, enter the Empowerment Zone portion of my story.

When I first learned HUD was sending us an Empowerment Zone and some of the $100 million was coming to my Sandtown neighborhood and that it could provide resources for new businesses, I knew I wanted to learn more. Sandtown and three other West Baltimore neighborhoods had what the government called a "Village Center," and there were also two

Village Centers on the Eastside that received funds. *Possibly*, I thought to myself, *I should become a business owner*. My rationale was I could get paid to do what I love. It sure made good sense to me!

As fate would have it, one day I received an invitation to interview for the public information job at the Baltimore Empowerment Zone Headquarters. I was elated over the possibilities of a new job with much better pay, citywide media access and the ability to still edit the community newspaper. And little did I know I was about to be asked to co-host a weekly radio show on Radio One Baltimore's WOLB 1010 AM, now in its 16th year.

Here's a very valuable lesson for young and old people alike: Show up! You never know what may happen; but first you gotta show up! They say showing up is 90% of the battle. What I've learned is it pays to show up. You never know who might *not* show up, like the first string guy, for example. And while he's busy thinking he can rest on his laurels, you can show up, step in, show out and replace him.

When you show up, you better position yourself for upcoming opportunities. But, you won't get the shot if you don't show up. And trust me when I tell you that for a long time I didn't show up. That's right. I was the guy who made commitments only to break them. I said I was going to do something but somehow, someway, fell just a little short. Hell, in short, I was a no-show. A brother you couldn't count on for anything except the hot air blowing from my mouth when I talked the talk but didn't back it up by walking the way. Then somehow I made a conscious decision to do something worthwhile with my life. I chose to nurture my gifts and talents. I chose to respect God and allow Him to teach me how to use that with which He had blessed me. I learned to show up and be a blessing, not a curse, to others.

The Empowerment Zone gig was right on time. It was the logical next step to grow my media presence beyond the confines of my 72-block community. Because business was a key component of the Empowerment Zone initiative, a number of programs were included that offered entrepreneurs and business owners different assistance opportunities. My personal goal was to learn as much as I could, and my aim was to milk it for every bit of knowledge I could get. I realized there were so many facets to running a business and I had to be versed in all of them. Of course, this meant knowing when to call in the professional. Whether the business issue was taxes, graphics, licensing, or what have you, I knew a good business owner knows how to find out who to go to for the right answer if he or she didn't know it him or herself. It's no different than President Obama. We all know the brother is bad and knows his shit. But he's still human just like you and me and doesn't know everything about everything. Albert Einstein didn't either for that matter. So President Obama has a talented Cabinet backing him that includes Eric Holder, Valerie Jarrett and Susan Rice, just to name a few.

I learned so much at the Empowerment Zone. My supervisor, Michael Preston, was an exceptional teacher who still advises me today. This cat showed me the ropes in marketing and business development and re-introduced me to the world of radio. And at that time I hadn't been on the air since I was a teenager and hanging out with my mentor and city school teacher Charlie Dugger. I saw things coming together in my life. I was learning a lot of good things at Empower Baltimore Management Corporation about media, marketing, the significance of relationships and integrity. And I was feeling that entrepreneurial bug more and more.

The work at the Empowerment Zone Headquarters was much like the work I did in Sandtown, except on a broader, citywide level. Instead of focusing only on Sandtown, my catchment area became larger, which was just fine with me. It was exactly what I needed to build my own media outlet. At this point I was co-hosting "Empower Hour" with Mike Preston every Tuesday on the radio, and I began building a name for myself. I also had my own show which immediately followed; I was able to find sponsors and ultimately began to create and further brand a rather popular name for myself in local radio.

Truthfully, the idea of starting a business had routinely crossed my mind. After all, I'm an entrepreneur by blood, meaning I'm always thinking of ways to make money doing what I love to do and am good at: Multi-Media and Public Relations. I certainly have the interest!

So I knew I wanted my own publication. After five years or so of being the editor/co-editor of the *Sandtown-Winchester ViewPoint*, it was clear I'd never be happy working for somebody else in media. I'd always be counting someone else's money and focused on how to make them even more money.

Point blank: I needed and wanted my own. I wanted fiduciary responsibility as well as the 'final say'.

You see, I saw how the community newspaper could make money with ads, but I didn't have the final say. And I knew people paid good money to get their ads in popular publications. To me, that was honest, good and consistent money. And again, I love making honest money. Quiet as it's kept, I love to shop. And that fetish ultimately fueled my desire to have my own media outlet.

Thank God for the patience, though. I learned you have to sweep somebody else's floor before you can sweep your own. Hence, the Empowerment Zone afforded me the spectacular opportunity to understand how my written and oral communication skills could yield a demand and handsome income if used properly. And, I was meeting more and more like-minded entrepreneurs who were following their dreams. I figured if I could combine my skill set with some new marketing expertise, I could quite possibly make a living for myself.

I also learned you have to learn the game before you can play the game. It's called paying one's dues or earning one's stripes. And that's exactly the route I'd suggest to any person attempting to master a craft. Start from the bottom up to ensure you have a strong appreciation for every facet of the operation and know how all of the parts work together for the whole. Doing this will teach you to respect all people no matter their occupation or station in life. And, in turn, it will humble you and show others you're a down-to-earth brother who doesn't have his nose stuck in the air.

By the way, I suggest young people work a multitude of gigs because each one is a valuable lesson. I can honestly say as a person trying to gain a foothold, each one of the fifty-plus jobs I've had taught me at least one thing: why I did not want that particular job as a career. That's significant because you wind up with an impressive body of experience in a litany of odd jobs that teach you about yourself, life, people and so much more. To me, that's the real learning necessary for success in any field. You've got to learn how things work from the ground up and inside and out. You have to learn people and their behavior. Business people study behavior and patterns all day long. They pay attention to trends. Most of all, you have to intimately learn and master yourself.

And that's just what I needed to learn: people, business and how to maximize my skill set. I wanted to know how to run my own profitable news outlet and how to provide advertisers with a compelling media outlet that effectively reached the masses. I wanted to know how to brand myself and my company on the web. I had an endless supply of questions to which I desperately needed answers. From workshops to seminars to specific classes, I came to focus on what I needed to do to make my own shop possible.

I started by doing my own a publication, *The North Avenue Review*, for six months. That publication was my first step toward making an entrepreneurial name for myself in print citywide. I also got an opportunity to delve into the world of print publishing. I gained a lot of respect for the black publishers out there, including those in Baltimore. They're a special breed of people with whom I've had some great relationships over the years.

Having been the editor of the Sandtown community newspaper since 1994, I knew the time had come for a broader reach. Besides, my work at the Empowerment Zone had opened my mind to broader possibilities. As my contract at the Empowerment Zone was coming to an end, my media career was blossoming. My reach had extended way past the 72-square blocks of Sandtown, and by 2002 I was constantly being invited on radio and television news shows.

Further, I was now writing for the now-120 year old *Afro* newspaper, the city's historic weekly. And I was writing for the *Baltimore Times*, also a black-owned newspaper but with only a 25-year history. *The Times* tends to focus mostly on positive stories whereby the *Afro* is more across-the-board, telling the good, the bad and all that's in the middle. And, I was also writing pieces for the *Final Call* newspaper, headquartered in Chicago. Yes, there's no doubt about it. My star was most definitely rising.

Making the Empowerment Zone Experience Work for Me

I'm so grateful for the body of knowledge I gained while working at Baltimore's Empowerment Zone. From a programmatic standpoint primarily focused on West and East Baltimore, the $100 million federally-funded Empowerment Zone brought with it much more than just money. It brought love. It brought decency. It helped people get back some of the self-respect they'd been stripped of by a system that seemed hell-bent on keeping them down. It brought together people in the community. It ushered in an era of forgiveness. And the captain of the ship, Diane Bell-McCoy, did a marvelous job to the best of her ability to ensure the money was allocated correctly, wisely and with lasting results. I should add at the end of the day, Baltimore's Empowerment Zone was a national model, and I was damn glad and proud to be a part of it.

The former President and CEO of Empower Baltimore Management Corporation, Bell-McCoy, is a very classy woman who makes you proud of black people. She can walk with kings and queens and yet is down-to-earth enough to hear an aspiring entrepreneur's dreams.

Needless to say, this woman has had a huge impact on my life. She always reminded me of one thing: Follow your heart. No matter what my question was, she invariably told me the same thing: Follow your heart. Hell, she said it so much to me I still hear it in my sleep. No joke.

And she said it with encouragement as opposed to with a tone that conveyed she just didn't want to really think of an answer. Well, I have followed my heart and it has taken me through some pretty interesting doors. And when I go through those doors, I'm simultaneously thinking news, business and politics.

Years later, I still say leaving Sandtown and going to work in beautiful downtown Baltimore was the best possible professional move I could have made. It was a stage of growth for me. A great yet simple lesson here is we have to be willing to leave our comfort zones to grow. Just like a young plant eventually outgrows its initial pot, at times we must be willing to move to larger post. Sometimes you just need a larger airport because your plane is growing and needs more room.

It wasn't like I hadn't worked downtown before. But I'd gone through a lot since I last worked downtown as a stockbroker trainee and as a waiter, making a lot of mistakes in the process. However, God has a way of turning things around if we allow Him. And that's what I did. I'm a living witness that God can use evil intended for bad, for good. I stopped doing many of the destructive things I was doing to myself. And to say the least, there were a lot of late nights as a waiter.

At this time in my life, I'd begun to learn and embrace humility. I'd become more grateful for everything. And that's why I constantly give God the praise and the glory because my way was looking neither pretty nor promising. However, if we keep God first, we can do anything. With God, failure is not an option.

Only God could have turned my ship around. Only God could have taken all of those good and bad experiences and turned them into something beautiful. You see, there were some very dark days prior to starting my business. I can also say, however, if you pray and persevere no matter what, and if you grow increasingly more obedient, God can transform an 'ugly' situation into a 'beautiful' one before you know it. And that's exactly what He did for me. So, without becoming too pastoral, I can truly say God has made my career and life possible, and for that and many other reasons, it is God

Almighty to whom I will forever give praise. After God, I praise my parents, my grandparents and even myself for having the guts to make a much-needed change in my life.

In short, I went to work at the Empowerment Zone as a public information specialist and while there fully realized my ultimate focus was to start my own business in media and in my now newfound love of public relations.

After all, there was no way I could work at the Empowerment Zone, assisting hundreds of business owners and entrepreneurs, and not empower myself at the same time. It dawned on me one day while I was working there not to lose sight of *why* I was there. Sure, being the best public relations specialist was a goal. However, the CEO kept us focused on 'what's next'. My 'what's next' was the vision of owning a business doing much of what I was doing at the Empowerment Zone and some of what I was increasingly doing politically.

I wanted to take my media and public relations skills and form my own entity, a Multimedia Marketing and Public Relations Firm. Granted, it might have been somewhat impossible, unrealistic or at the least extremely difficult; but, that's unequivocally what I wanted to do at the time. I thought I could generate enough income between news advertisers and public relations clients to handle my bills. Mind you, this was 2002, George W. Bush was president and the economy was still good. But unless you've been living under a rock and asleep like Rip Van Winkle to boot, you know this country soon experienced its worst economic climate since the Great Depression of 1929.

And that's just where the words of Nate Chapman come to mind: He told me if I could grow a business in that kind of economic climate, I could essentially do anything. He told me I was doing something special and to keep going. That meant a lot to me – hearing those encouraging words from an icon who had mentored me since 1985. And so, pursue it I did.

I've found if you stick with something, you usually become good at it. The more I wrote the more power I had. The more I could express myself on paper, the more I found myself becoming a much larger and stronger voice for black people.

Over time, my regular newspaper editorial started touching people and eventually developed into The Glover Report, a prominent feature on www.bmorenews.com today. The more I wrote, the more media opportunities came my way, including interviews at Maryland Public Television, which was home of another mentor, Mr. Charles Robinson.

If I were asked how it all happened, I'd simply say one thing led to another. I just kept showing up for opportunities wherever they occurred, and thus I began gaining a solid journalism reputation.

In time I was in full-gear. I'd built a mini-media empire in Baltimore. I had my own show on FM ('One Mic', WEAA 88.9 FM, Morgan State University), another show on AM ("Empower Hour", Radio One Baltimore's WOLB 1010 AM), my editorial subscribership continued to grow, my television appearances on Baltimore's NBC affiliate (WBAL TV 11) had multiplied and my email newsletter subscribership continued growing, too.

In the process, I started getting calls for quotes on a number of political issues around the area known as DMV – D.C., Maryland and Northern Virginia. The quote seekers included reporters from the *Washington Post, Washington Times, Baltimore Sun* and my favorite, the *Montgomery Gazette.*

Why were they calling? I think the world has come to know I speak unapologetically from my heart on matters about black people and speak prayerfully with a peculiar love for an otherwise forsaken community. Reporters who call apparently are looking for a black perspective from a man with a whole lot of passion for black progress who has a little something to say. At least, that's certainly what I aim to give them.

For instance, after a few years of the Sandtown gig, I concluded a black agenda was indeed necessary if I was going to continue doing this kind of work. There had to be a set of goals that I decided must be simple, doable and tangible. And I knew the black community needed to embrace it for it to work. Therefore, I had to be on-point. For me, the black agenda that few can argue against includes: (1) public education, (2) black businesses/employment, (3) services for ex-offenders (especially given that over 40% of America's prison population is comprised of black men), (4) universal access to healthcare and (5) affordable housing.

I think if these five agenda items are embraced collectively by black leaders, including businessmen, pastors, entertainers (particularly given they increasingly give political opinions) and elected officials, we can crack this nut that first Walter Rodney and later Dr. Manning Marable called the 'under-development' of black people.

And mind you, black leaders cannot go it alone. It will take committed white people who are intent on doing the right thing. Too often, white folks want to come in and tell black people what to do and how to do it as opposed to first listening to black people and understanding the given challenges. As black people are better able to help themselves, and as white Americans start treating us with the respect we deserve and allowing us a fair shot at good jobs, quality education and other opportunities, the more of a blessing Black Americans can be to America The Beautiful, and the fewer prisons we'll need. But there has to be buy-in. I'm not sure, however, that such buy-in exists. Former Maryland Attorney General Doug Gansler, in my book, is the first politician statewide that I know of to become vocal about pushing education over incarceration.

Unfortunately, our leadership in the black community is so frazzled that fighting for black people is a dying art form. Further, without leadership and vision, the people are lost. The days of the powerful leaders from the 1960s are long gone, I'm afraid. Instead, today New Jack politicians with the accoutrements of success and noticeable character voids often seem to permeate the scene. All the while, black people are being bombarded from all sides and don't know who to trust or which way to go. Preachers are flip-flopping. Black elected officials are flip-flopping. The condition of the people is so rough in the black community at times that even a blind man can see if black folks don't soon get it together, our people, our history and our rich, rich legacy of earth-shattering accomplishments will become virtually extinct.

Rarely talked about in mainstream media, the glaring reality is a major part of the reason for the decimation of the black family is the burgeoning prison industrial complex. It's legalized slavery and produces billions of dollars in profit, for mostly white American stockholders, annually. And black men alone comprise 44% of the prison population with too many doing time for non-violent drug offenses.

The American prison system incarcerates more people at a higher rate than any nation on earth. Add in the fact that black males are the primary clientele in these prisons, and I'm particularly peeved and wholeheartedly in search of a drastic change to that equation. It is annihilating the black family, at minimum.

Everybody and their momma knows it costs more to incarcerate a person than to educate a person, and that it's easier to build a good citizen than reform a wounded one. However, that doesn't change the minds of the people who benefit from this very successful American industry. They're too greedy to stop this prison pipeline, and my people are cannon fodder, or mere wood in the fireplace. And trust and believe, I have a major problem with that. Where America once had a black dilemma heightened by the protests of the 60s, an onslaught of illegal drugs and prisons soon gave the nation a solution that would catch on like wildfire.

Clearly the black community needs vision. We must re-embrace that black people working together and building on small victories can, in fact, live a better quality of life and better add to the well-being of this nation as in the days of Tulsa,

Oklahoma's Black Wall Street where hundreds of black businesses flourished together. Even more, we should be passing this mindset on to our children. If there is indeed hope, my prayer is the major issues facing Black America will finally be addressed. Those issues include depression, substance abuse, being under-educated and underemployed, single-parent households, the number of abortions young black girls and women have and over-incarceration.

There are also health disparities that are wreaking havoc in Black America, including heart disease, cancer, HIV/AIDS and diabetes. If President Barack Obama has done nothing by name for blacks, we can certainly say The Affordable Care Act, more commonly referred to as "Obamacare," has been a blessing that directly impacts black people in positive ways. Because of a lack of health insurance, black people tend to flood emergency rooms, while many people of other races have primary care physicians to treat them. But Obamacare is helping to change that. Let me just add, I am very aware that there are tons of poor whites in America.

Clearly, being under-educated is a huge issue – and not just in Black America. It's a damned and crying shame that we continue spending billions of dollars on war abroad while our children are increasingly lagging behind their counterparts in other countries. America's public school system is ranked 16th in the world. That is absolutely, fundamentally backwards. We invest in our war machine to ensure we have the best guns and ammunition, but we won't invest in the best libraries, books or the most up-to-date technology for our children. And we won't pay our teachers respectable salaries but instead force them to endure ridiculously high student-teacher ratios, in some cases to purchase their own school supplies and we house them in buildings that should have been razed years ago. Now that's bullshit to the nth degree!

We should be directing corporate welfare to the citizens with the goal of building a better-educated and more responsible citizenry. However, to deny one's own people the fruit of their labor is to commit national suicide. To fail to ensure that all Americans realize their academic potential is the equivalent of treason in my book. For only a segment to benefit off the work of the masses is wrong and just not smart. And then people wonder why the end result is mayhem. Truth be told, everybody must be able to work and feed their families. And given all of the Ivy League degrees floating around in America, we should be able to feed all Americans, not to mention factoring in our excessive gross national waste.

Hence, twenty years of writing and reporting stories, especially those about or affecting African-Americans, has given me a unique perspective. From the crack house to the White House, my forte is the black community. I'm concerned with every aspect of the black experience from pre-natal care to funeral arrangements, from kindergartens classes to exercises classes for senior citizens. I love my people, and I've made it my business to try to write stories about them, to try to uplift them and to call out those who willfully and maliciously try to hurt them – whether those folk are white or, as is sadly sometimes the case, black themselves.

I've covered graduations, after-school programs, mentoring programs, sports teams and churches. My team has even broadcasted live radio shows from inside the halfway house on Greenmount Avenue to showcase potential employees who were on their way home. As a result, I've found what's critical to the further development of black people is the same as for every other group. Black people need to be healthy, have decent, good-paying jobs and affordable, more than simply habitable roofs over their heads. Food, shelter and clothing are the basics, but black people need education and recreation just like everybody else. And black people deserve to be treated like human beings. Anything else is purely uncivilized. Hence, to live in a city where there is more money put on law enforcement and increasingly less on recreation centers creates an even bigger death trap for our youth. This must change. And the ancestors would agree.

Defining The Black Agenda

From my perspective, any black leader worth his or her start can embrace this agenda. After all, it's hardly rocket science. It's about giving the people what they need: (1) public education; (2) black businesses/employment; (3) services for ex-offenders; (4) affordable housing; and (5) universal access to healthcare. When black people have a better quality of life and when black children are succeeding in schools across the country like never before, then there will be a manifestation of the unconditional love to which I'm accustomed. Until then, there's plenty of work to do to get us there, and I invite anybody on the same page to give me a call so maybe we can work together.

Having said that, the time had come for me to start my very own business. Thus, on August 9, 2002, I took another step on my entrepreneurial journey and named the parent company DMGlobal Marketing and Public Relations. I named our flagship website www.bmorenews.com. I wanted my own shop where I could run the show using my own vision. At this point, I had already tried *SandtownLive.com*, but that proved to be too parochial in scope. I had also tried my hand at *The North Avenue REVIEW* publication for six months but soon realized I wanted a news website with a citywide scope. I also realized I needed another arm of the business specifically for servicing clients in need of marketing and PR services. Why? News alone doesn't generate income. Advertisers do! So, DMGlobal was the arm by which I came to serve a variety of clients, including non-profits, lawyers, corporations and the like who were in need of PR and marketing – people who wanted to get the word out about their enterprise, program or event. If anybody can get the word out, believe me you I can!

Thus, this was the beginning of the next stage of my life. Needless to say, starting a business wasn't the easiest thing in the world to do. However, God placed some great people and mentors in my life, like Mr. Raymond V. Haysbert, Sr., then-CEO of the Forum Caterers. He's a perfect example of the people I emulate. A former Tuskegee Airmen and former CEO of Parks Sausage Company, he passed away a few years ago but was my first long-term advertiser. In him I was blessed to have not just a customer but also a mentor and a friend. He's referred to as Maryland's "Dean of Business" because he had tons of experience and didn't mind sharing his knowledge with serious-minded folks, including me. He especially didn't mind discussing his mistakes, and that took confidence and guts.

Ray's words, "Go for the low-hanging fruit," still ring in my ears today. In other words, attain some small victories because they eventually lead to larger successes.

Chapter 5
Black Political Economy and the Need for Black Entrepreneurship

Individuals like Mr. Haysbert are a constant reminder to me of our vast potential as a people. Though he had his share of failures, his life and legacy as a successful entrepreneur serve as a vivid reminder that just as civil rights are important to black progress, so are so-called "Silver Rights." Haysbert, a Republican, insisted we understand both are important to our onward progress and survival. We need civil rights, he argued, but we also need to make money. He constantly reiterated to his students that the struggle for equality must involve economics. To him, civil rights mean nothing without Silver Rights, or the ability to access money and wealth.

He insisted his students understand we had an obligation to become successful in business. He also wanted us to understand we must parlay our political power into economic advantages for our community, and nobody else can do it for us but us. The very fact that he was a Republican in a nine-to-one Democratic town and yet was so popular demonstrated how far he was willing to go to show us we can't afford to think inside the box at any juncture along the journey.

Haysbert's political affiliation was forever indicative to me that we must think for ourselves regardless of our political party. Too often, blacks allow outside entities like newspapers to define us. Armed with wisdom from a Baltimore legend and many others including my dad, I hungered to learn as much as I could about business *and* politics. You see, because Ray was so successful people didn't care what party he was in. In fact, his political affiliation demonstrated to us *how* to use power. Put differently, insanity is doing the same thing over and over and expecting a different outcome. Time and again blacks have been fully invested in the Democratic Party, but it has been the Democratic Party that has consistently taken the black vote for granted while giving very little in return. Thus, if nothing changes, nothing changes. So we have to do something different.

Over time I learned commerce and trade, essential to progress in any community, can provide great opportunities for people to work together. Everybody loves to make money. This is so in Africa and Black America just like anywhere else in the world. Further, given a trillion dollars in annual disposable income in the black community in the U.S., along with Africa's vast natural resources, I'm as about as pro-African-business as anybody else. Like Randall Robinson, Marcus Garvey, Louis Sullivan and others, I want to see more economic cooperation among blacks worldwide. Like Frazier Mathis of GlobalVessels.org, I think African-Americans can help lead the way. W.E.B. DuBois and Kwame Nkrumah also come to mind. Like these great leaders, I know as black people learn to do for self, the better off we'll be. The more we take our own destiny by the horns, the more likely we'll succeed in an ever-globalizing economy.

I'm an avid believer in being proactive and doing for self, and I believe this is one of the most important things we must teach our children. I think, for instance, entrepreneurship is an essential part of any community's progress and therefore must be a top priority in any black Agenda. This is why I'm so very attracted to the success of the people in Tulsa; they demonstrated what can be accomplished when we *do* believe in ourselves and work together. For me, Black Wall Street in Tulsa that was burned and bombed to the ground by a mob of angry whites will forever serve as perpetual evidence of what's possible when we work together. The bottom line is every community has a need for an economic engine, and entrepreneurs tend to lead the way. Business drives America, Asia and Europe. And business certainly drives Africa. Hence, this is the area in which I aim to thrive and make my most significant contribution to the cause.

So it's my hope that increasingly more blacks worldwide see the possibilities afforded by entrepreneurship and doing for ourselves. It's important to me for more and more of us to see ourselves as a part of that economic engine driving the global economy – not just as employees. *Au contraire!* We can be employers! We can be the boss! Giving our propensity to outspend other Americans, we must also master how to garner our one trillion dollars in annual disposable income such that those dollars circulate multiple times in the black community before leaving.

In my lifetime, I've come to view entrepreneurship as a viable mechanism for a lot of people, even if it's just part-time. The more I read, the more I realize how Africans in America have been hustlin' since slave ship days. Truth be told, black folks in the U.S. have always been entrepreneurial, whether they were free black men who owned businesses or slaves who had side hustles on Sundays.

As the son of entrepreneurs, it's second nature for me to have an enterprise in the works. I've been around entrepreneurs my entire life and have learned from them there's a certain independence that comes with owning a business. There is a certain sense of liberation that comes with doing for self. Indeed, the mindset of entrepreneurs can't be found anywhere else, as they're Olympians in their own right. Ms. Chillie, owner of the Odyssey Lounge, comes to mind; she was a best friend to my father.

I think doing business for self is totally empowering, especially for challenged communities like mine. That's why I'm always encouraging business owners to hang in there. It's exactly why the Black Wall Street Series is so critical to our mission at Bmorenews. It's not easy being an entrepreneur, but it can be done successfully. And I figure the more we become successful entrepreneurs, no matter how difficult the task, the better off we'll be. After all, the entrepreneur is indeed the lifeline of this country! All we need to do is to work together.

The concept of running one's own business is far from new to the African-American community. Heck, my maternal grandmother, Mary A. Murray, sold Stanley products until she passed away in her 80's. I believe there's nothing like mastering an industry and parlaying that passion into a profitable entrepreneurial empire that helps somebody along the way.

Black Wall Street Tulsa is that quintessential model of the type of business wealth I envision for today's black community. Tulsa demonstrated the 'cooperative economics' mindset that's necessary for such success. Prior to being nearly decimated in 1921, it served as a shining example of the greatness black people can achieve when everyone plays his or her part. Durham, the home of North Carolina Mutual Insurance Company, and Richmond, Va., home of Jackson Ward's Maggie Walker, also had Black Wall Streets where black business was the order of the day. In Brooklyn, N.Y., the area was called Weeksville. Baltimore had Historic Pennsylvania Avenue and Old Town Mall; Baltimore is also home to the oldest black family business in America, Locks Funeral Home which has a history that goes back to the 1700s. Even more, Africville, Nova Scotia, saw similar economic activity amongst blacks in Canada. These examples demonstrate that blacks can successfully operate businesses.

I believe if we can return to playing love songs and loving ourselves even amidst racism, we will realize we have everything we need for success. I believe if we work together there is no goal we cannot achieve. And I think the same is true for any other community anywhere in the world.

My upbringing taught me that God helps those who help themselves. If we get out there and work hard with a plan, just like Reginald F. Lewis and countless others did, we can make things happen, be successful and ensure everybody eats. We've done it before and can do it again.

For blacks in America, if we could just parlay the trillion dollars in disposable income we generate annually into political influence and vote strategically just as the Jews do, we could better determine our collective destiny. If we could just overcome infighting, jealousy, stinginess and entitlement, we'd have a fighting chance. People from South Korea do it. People from India do it. And so can blacks.

However, because we have not mastered the 'money and politics' game, we repeatedly get the short end of the stick. The only time politicians visit black folk in Baltimore, or statewide for that matter, is when they need our vote. Instead of answering our demands and addressing our issues, they usually tell us about somebody else's agenda, which proves we're not using our political capital wisely. It happens election after election.

I think we can establish an even more progressive black community in the DMV area and anywhere else there are masses of black folks if we become more attentive to the issues and if we get better at understanding the candidates. We must demand what we need up front, request promises in writing and hold candidates accountable. Too often, we let politicians of all races 'skate' on us without holding their feet to the fire. When we don't keep an eye on them, they do what they want. That's not a scenario for progress but instead is a recipe for failure. If you look around Baltimore's black community today, you'll know what I mean. The number of blacks in Baltimore is constantly going down.

Hence, the black vote is less and less important in a town where blacks once held a lot more power. Though incredibly valuable, the black vote is often disrespected and taken for granted. When black politicians don't do right, they must be addressed and reminded of their duty. Through my work I seek to protect the black vote and its historical significance. People like Fannie Lou Hamer and Clarence Mitchell, Jr. believed we deserve no less.

I think we've forgotten the value of our vote and that for a long time we didn't even have one. Education can change that, so I try to use Bmorenews and our other platforms to teach people a lot of things we should know, including the importance and sacredness of the black vote.

Too many of us can't name our elected officials, which is extremely dangerous. When we don't know who we're voting for, we have the potential of empowering people who don't have our best interests at heart. Nothing in politics or life could be more foolish. If we don't know what to do with our vote, you best believe somebody else does.

We must better use our vote to push our agenda and to force elected officials to serve our interests, including the interests of Minority Business Enterprises (MBEs). Those who don't comply should be voted out. Plain and simple. Marion Barry told me that years ago, and I have never forgotten his words. We must always remember the black and white ancestors who fought and died for people to have the right to vote and honor their efforts by becoming intelligently and actively engaged in the political process at all levels. It is fundamental. We must make our vote count for something meaningful. I believe as we master the worlds of business and politics, we can begin turning around our communities. Right now, too much of Black America is in turmoil.

Thus, understanding the inter-relationship of politics and economics is a most critical lesson for the black community. I think by better parlaying our politics into economic growth and development, i.e. jobs, we'll reap a better economic benefit. But, it takes commitment, integrity and selflessness. It requires the necessary work to achieve the necessary results. And, it takes leadership that can make employment opportunities readily available for the most disenfranchised people, including ex-offenders and people in recovery. In my opinion, people like Marion Barry and Maynard Jackson are strong examples of the kind of black political leadership we need today.

Clearly, Black America has an unemployment problem, which is typically twice as high as that of white America. Yet if we would better pool our resources, our businesses and our political power would be much stronger and, at the end of the day, our families and our communities would be much stronger, too. We'd be able to better facilitate empowering options to our people if we work together. This means the politician, the preacher, the business person, the academic and the community activist. When we can all work together selflessly for a common goal, we will all win.

This is a bit about me, my work and my passion. I have an undying commitment to our people because I think we deserve the best. And so I use my gifts and talents to help do my part to help us find some daylight. America is a big corporation. I recognize that. It's a business. And so Black America must learn from the past, pool our resources and become a better player in the political game and the business market. The focus of my business is to help small businesses and corporations alike tap into the global market, and my main tool is Bmorenews.com.

Chapter 6
My Business is My Daily Passion

To say the least, DMGlobal Marketing and PR, the parent company of www.bmorenews.com, is very much my passion. No day is the same. Each one is unique. Further, I am just incredibly attracted to the notion of taking my destiny by the horns, following my passion and in the process helping some people along the way.

To me, entrepreneurship is taking absolutely nothing and turning it into an Egyptian pyramid, an entity that becomes a proven and respected tool for the broader community. That's my hope for Bmorenews.com. The news and information portal my team birthed in Baltimore in August 2002 has become a noteworthy voice for the underrepresented in our world. The parent company, DMGlobal, Marketing and PR, services a litany of clients while providing affordable marketing and public relations solutions. Suffice it to say, Bmorenews and DMGlobal are like my children, key components of my purpose for living. I pray the work we've done speaks for itself.

Each and every day I'm prepared and motivated to take my business higher, without resting on yesterday's laurels. I'm determined to see my business continue succeeding. Critical in ensuring that is effectively branding Bmorenews so it gets embedded even harder in the minds of people near and far. Along the way, I'm helping a lot of people, and that's really a beautiful thing. And, truth be told, sometimes the best service I can give is educating people with tidbits of wisdom. Providing free education doesn't pay a dime, but it's necessary for our overall success as a people and is the right thing to do. Sharing and teaching and uplifting are part of the investment I've committed to make to help move my people forward. And, let me tell you, I sometimes struggle with this because people can be so ungrateful and selfish, concerned with only themselves. Likewise, many never offer a hand to somebody else, no matter how much assistance and love they're blessed with. Some wouldn't help Jesus. Nonetheless, I've found it necessary to take time to show people a better way even when they act foolishly because clearly the good outweighs the bad. Even more, I know many, many people helped me, and, at times, I wasn't the easiest fella to work with either.

Entrepreneurship and service to others are in my blood. From sun up to sun down, I was born for this. This is what I do! I assist lawyers, authors, celebrities, writers, corporations, non-profits and politicians by disseminating customized messages to their target market. I help them brand themselves, particularly by utilizing the World Wide Web. Most of my clients are in the DMV area, but I have also been afforded the opportunity to serve some national clients in Washington D.C., New York, Los Angeles, Chicago and Cleveland. Internationally, I've done some reporting from abroad and have worked on a few accounts for Global Vessels while in Ethiopia and Tanzania. I learned people are people no matter where you are. That's because the essential concept of business is universal: Do right by people and they will do right by you.

My hope is that during our twelve-year-tenure our beloved flagship, Bmorenews.com, has garnered a respectable name. It is the Mothership, the record, the library and the electronic catalog that has told many otherwise unknown stories and has boosted many business client's "Google-ability." From our stats, I've come to know Bmorenews is certainly more than a website. It's a movement with empowering the community as its mission. From business to politics to community and entertainment, we cover news from an Afrocentric standpoint that is unequivocally and unapologetically black.

We absolutely adore reporting on black entrepreneurs and emerging black politicos. We love telling the story of self-empowerment that would otherwise not get told, the stories often overlooked by mainstream media. To me, there is nothing sweeter than seeing people get the exposure they deserve and knowing we helped make that happen. It brings me great joy to know we helped lift a business' profile. I absolutely love when that happens, when we help others succeed.

I pray this book about my journey as an entrepreneur touches people in a positive way – whether the reader is a young black boy from the inner-city, an aspiring journalist, an aspiring entrepreneur, a politico or none of the above. Just know that when we tap into our calling, when we tap into our purpose we are well on our way. It's going to take some effort, but who knows? It might be easier than you think. I just know you won't find out if you never try. You'll never get an answer if you never knock on the door. So, go for it! Like my dad used to say, "If you get out there and try, somebody might see you and help you."

My friend KC Carter once told me he's not praying and working for blessings just for him. And I feel the same. I'm praying and working for an overflow so blessings spill over into my neighbor's house, the community next door, the city up the coast and to people all over the world.

Because I am a black man in North America, I really hope this book encourages other brothers to do some constructive things with their lives, beginning with seizing a well-rounded education. I hope this book enlightens African-American males in cities across America to the possibilities that lie ahead if they just persevere. I want young black men, in particular, to know anything is possible, even in America. I've seen life from the top and life from the bottom – from Southeast D.C. to East Baltimore to East New York to the Middle East to East Africa. All I can say is we should aim for balance in everything we do. Be consistent and one day a break-through will come. I believe that: *real talk*!

As I have pondered this book's release, *The Autobiography of Malcolm X* has repeatedly come to mind. I was 15 when I first read his autobiography in a mere three days, and I can say it changed my world, so to speak. His words expanded and broadened my scope, and that is exactly my hope for the readers of this book: to be inspired and to know that with God all things are possible, no matter how bleak things might seem at the present. I specifically want the black entrepreneur to know a special blessing awaits those who are faithful.

Another great inspiration for me is the late Rev. Dr. Martin Luther King, Jr., the primary reason I attended Morehouse

College. Like many of you, I have been blessed by his earth-shattering oratories and am in awe of his extensive list of accomplishments nationally and internationally.

And so, just as Malcolm's and Dr. King's writings and speeches have inspired me, I pray this book inspires some young black males because they are the most ostracized demographic in America. Black men are the obvious underdog in America and clearly the most endangered species in America. I want young black men to be aware and to be encouraged. Life can get better. Indeed it can, but we must have a plan and work the plan.

Too many black men are in prison, adjudicated, involved with illegal drugs or not with their children. It is a plight worse than slavery for far too many who look like me. A key concern of mine is reducing the numbers of black men in the prison industrial complex in America, in which too many play a starring, and often recurring, role Thus, I am very interested in seeing more young black men tap into their purpose and avoid this seemingly ubiquitous trap. Having spoken in prisons to young inmates, I know far too many just need a little help and a little love for things to turn around. I've seen progress first-hand far too many times to lose hope.

I also hope this book sparks some fire for emerging journalists of all races who may find it difficult to grow a career; I pray they are bitten by the entrepreneurial bug to consider a career as a media entrepreneur like myself. I actually think the electronic and digital age has created more opportunities for journalists than ever – an immediate segue into entrepreneurship. I certainly hope to inspire more entrepreneurship among the masses with my book. When people are doing what they really love, the world is a better place. Quite often, that means opening one's own shop. The same applies to all people regardless of race. When we do what we love and are good at it, nothing can be better except passing on the encouragement to as many deserving people as possible.

Entrepreneurship is a risk not meant for most. However, it is a viable option for those who, like a championship boxer, are prepared to go the distance. So I also pray this book provides encouragement to the visionary business risk-takers, a.k.a. the entrepreneur. As the child of two entrepreneurs, I cannot imagine not working for myself because nothing else seems to fit.

I just cannot fathom the thought of doing media without being an owner. I'd rather be in a position of power than not. First, I appreciate the latitude of making my own editorial decisions. Second, I've seen countless media personalities in my twenty years end up on the street on their butts when just minutes before they had the world at their feet. So how did they fail? In too many cases they neglected to build their own media entity while enjoying six-figure salaries, and when they faced being laid off they had no exit strategy. My older cousin, Jamal Hakim, said he learned the importance of having an exit strategy from the Honorable Elijah Muhammad. Jamal also tells me frequently that my dad inspired him to be an entrepreneur, which speaks to the continuum of progress into which more of us need to tap. His brother, Andre Glover, concurs; Andre, too, is an entrepreneur. We have successful examples and nuggets of wisdom all around us. We simply need to find them and soak up as much of their wisdom as possible.

Personally, I think if you don't build your own dream you'll eventually help build someone else's. I don't like the sound of that. It's not cool at all. It doesn't gel in my spirit to work to build somebody else's dream because I have my own. What's more, I happen to think I can do anything for myself and be successful. Let me be clear. We should always learn from others, and this sometimes means working for other people. Heck, I worked over 50 different jobs. However, when I opened the doors to DMGlobal, I knew then as I know now it really encapsulates much of what I love and have been called to do.

I also hope you, the reader, are inspired to do absolutely anything you put your mind to, including writing a book, running your own business or both. I believe once a person accepts his or her gifts, passion and God-ordained mission in life, absolutely nothing at all can stop or deter that person from accomplishing his or her goal. Believe me as we tap into our purpose, we will come to fall in love with ourselves all over again.

The great leaders in the world all understand the value of ownership. Like Billie Holiday sang in "God Bless the Child", the heavens will bless you if you go out and get *your own*. Entrepreneurship, when successful, can translate into a media career or the music or book publishing industry. While it carries a big risk, entrepreneurship is incredibly liberating and can extend one's reach and footprint into whatever industry one chooses. It can also extend people's careers by empowering them to seize their own destinies rather than waiting for others to shape, guide or define them. Even more, I believe God reserves special blessings for entrepreneurs because He respects how they envision goals and make things happen to achieve them.

To me, ownership or being an employer is worth the risk, and just like Reginald F. Lewis, I have the audacity to think I can do it. After all, renting doesn't have the same value as home ownership. Of course, we all have to start somewhere, and before I bought a house, I rented a room. Similarly, I've found working for somebody else teaches us very important lessons, lessons future business owners really need to know. Still, at the end of the day I want my name on the building and the company checkbook.

I'm just saying ultimately everyone has a calling, and if you're like me, yours is not nine to five. My calling revolves around full-time entrepreneurship, and, sometimes, it seems there aren't enough hours in the day. Sometimes I look up and can't believe the time or how long I've been working.

I realize I must follow my calling because to do otherwise would be self-betrayal. I firmly believe we have to follow our dreams no matter how challenging. Without following our dreams, I don't think we can have peace because we'll wonder what could have been. You know, the old 'woulda, shoulda, coulda.' I don't fancy that scenario. I don't want to wonder what could have been, so the only way for me to find peace is to follow the vision God has given me.

This entrepreneurial journey has included my passion for politics, or the process of determining who gets what, when they get it and where they get it. I would say understanding the interrelationship of politics and economics, the allocation of the world's finite resources, is the crux of my personal mission. I'm one who appreciates a black president. Even more, I appreciate an educated black voting bloc that is goal-oriented and understands how to use political influence for the economic development of the black community.

Often we need to do what we have to do until we can do what we want to do. I've just always thought the best way for me has been ownership: owning my own media enterprise and creating my own deals and opportunities. There's nothing like it! If my mom were alive today, she would concur. Remember, she insisted all of her children become homeowners versus renters, and all four of us did. Additionally, I was the kid who chose business ownership, just as she and my father had.

So, I urge you to consider being the one who signs the paycheck versus the one who simply cashes it. Think big! Think like a business owner. Think like a visionary.

Let me be the first to say every day at DMGlobal and Bmorenews has not been easy, to say the least. It's peaks and valleys. Even so, God has provided for me and mine every single day without fail. And some days he provided for me through the kindness of others. For instance, on the few days when quitting seemed easiest, invariably someone called me out the blue and told me to keep doing what I was doing. The caller would also say the money would come. Soon I stopped thinking of quitting and marched onward, abandoning all negative thoughts of forgetting about my dreams.

This book proudly examines how I built www.bmorenews.com into a news and information portal with visitors from two hundred nations around the world to the tune of a million hits per month, pushed a five-point agenda before local, state and national audiences, survived the worst economy in modern times, worked with political leaders to push black issues, covered five other nations and visited the Obama White House more than twenty times. Mine is the story of sacrifices made and pains endured for the sake of following my dream because, regardless of the challenges, nothing could deter me from my goal of being a media entrepreneur.

It should be obvious by now I never really wanted a typical job but instead was always driven toward entrepreneurship. From selling newspapers to cutting grass, there's something about getting paid for self-initiated work that I find incredibly sexy. Think of the woman (or man) you consider just too sexy for words, and that's the way I feel about creating my own way to make money without having to punch anybody's clock or stress about whether heavy traffic makes my lunch hour extend beyond the allotted sixty minutes. Today, my goal is to better grow my enterprise, and I'm determined to succeed.

Running DMGlobal and Bmorenews are my calling, and I believe the industry called me. You know how some people say they were called to preach, or they were led to do this, that or the other? Sometimes, when it's all said and done, they realize they just jumped out there and did what they wanted to, without having that sense of being called or without urging from others. Well, I say running DMGlobal and Bmornews are my calling because when I reflect over my life, people kept asking me to stand up and read this or stand up and recite that, requests that date to Sunday School and elementary school. They kept asking, and I kept delivering – going back to when I helped do the morning announcements at Matthew Henson Elementary School #29. Media and business are my life – with a twist of politics, another of my callings.

And speaking of politics, an elder reminded me that the political landscape out of which I was born makes my story most interesting. I was born in Baltimore one hundred years after the Thirteenth Amendment abolished slavery. I was born just four months after my hero, Malcolm X, was assassinated and just over a month after I was born, the Nineteen Sixty-five Voting Rights Act was enacted. I was born at a time when the black nation was as strong as ever, in Baltimore and in other majority-black cities across America.

I have been reminded I was born in a city that was certainly aware of its black citizens. Even more, I've come to know how the black citizenry was keen on politics. Between 1830 and 1860, Baltimore had the largest number of free blacks in the nation. Couple this with a very strong list of powerful black Marylanders like Harriet Tubman and Frederick Douglass, and it's plain to see Baltimore has been terribly meaningful in black folks' fight for freedom and equality in America. Baltimore has also been meaningful in terms of black entrepreneurship.

One cannot forget the efforts of the Baltimore NAACP or the Baltimore branch of the Black Panther Party. They produced a litany of freedom fighters and caused Baltimore to shine, despite its history of segregated housing and inequitable public education. Baltimore has always opened its doors to the black entrepreneur and been recognized as a place where a black man came to succeed.

Essentially, Bmorenews.com was created to shed light on the strengths and courage of black people in Baltimore. Sure, Bmorenews.com celebrates our beloved Pennsylvania Avenue and its musical tradition. However, what's more important to this conversation are the contributions of Baltimoreans like Tom Smith, Thurgood Marshall and Kweisi Mfume, people who helped push black empowerment. The Goon Squad, a group of black community and religious leaders, also comes to mind. So, here's to continued reporting on a long legacy of political, business and social achievements in Baltimore that highlight the city and blacks in America as a whole. My hope is that Bmorenews can make a similarly spirited contribution and help improve life for people of color in America – beginning in my own backyard.

While times have indeed changed, Bmorenews must still carry the blood-stained banner, especially for those who cannot fight for themselves. And part of that mission involves reminding people of the strong, black tradition in Baltimore, reminding people of all of the great things that have happened for us in Baltimore and reminding them about how Baltimore was a national leader in the struggle. And yes, my ultimate hope is that Baltimore can once again symbolize black empowerment. While the players have changed, the fight is pretty much the same. And so, we carry on with the hope of making a positive difference in the world.

Chapter 7
Open for Business

Twelve years ago, after working my last job as a public information specialist at Baltimore's one hundred million dollar federally-funded Empowerment Zone under the tutelage of Baltimore's Queen of Transformation, Diane Bell-McCoy, I took a severance package, paid off my house and some other bills and opened up shop.

Empower Baltimore Management Corporation was responsible for managing the funds that led to business development and expansion, homeownership and employment in two East Baltimore communities and four West Baltimore communities.

As I've said, Sandtown-Winchester was one of the communities, so when a business development officer from the Empowerment Zone spoke at our Sandtown Community Center about entrepreneurship, bells went off in my head and I had to learn more. My dad used to always say when we take a step towards God, He takes a step towards us, and His steps are bigger. So I got my butt to that meeting, and God took it from there.

After talking to the business development officer, I quickly realized opening a business involved a lot of work. Granted, I'd worked in my father's funeral service operation all of my life and had also worked a cornucopia of different jobs, but suffice it to say I was clueless about running my own business.

I learned quickly, for instance, I needed a business plan, a living, breathing document that's always subject to modification. I also learned to stay focused on what I do and how I do it versus constantly monitoring my opposition. I learned to play to my strengths, to stick to what I do best and to hire the appropriate professionals to do that which I can't but need for my business to thrive.

In essence, I learned to pay attention to the advice of seasoned professionals and to implement their instructions. I think every entrepreneur must understand a very basic premise: devise a system to profitably deliver a service and/or product to the marketplace in the most cost-effective manner possible. For me, this ultimately means not doing any harm to man or the land in the process.

I encourage all entrepreneurs to get as many good mentors as they can because successful people will often share their pearls of wisdom. But understand it's pretty senseless to ask professionals for advice and neglect to apply it.

Here's something interesting. Raymond V. Haysbert, the late Chair of Park's Sausages, and I were talking once and discovered we both jot down notes in a notebook; I have filled up many notebooks over the years. Since that day, I've realized successful people share some common traits and success breeds certain habits, just as failure does. So, I unabashedly emulate successful people and, as I get older and wiser, pay even closer attention to what success looks like. Knowing one's self, one's abilities, one's limitations and one's faith can also lead to success. So, remember to get a notebook and write down your thoughts. If you're like me, you have a lot of them because there is absolutely no way you can remember everything.

Before I branched out on my own, I was at a turning point in my life. I was seriously pondering my future and ultimately the future of those around me because I knew the Empower Baltimore job wasn't going to last forever. Honestly, I was interested in working there for one main reason: entrepreneurship. I wanted to run my own business doing what I love to do. I wanted it so bad I could taste it. Finally, my ship had come. Here it was 2002 and I was presented with a choice, and I chose to go to work for myself. I'm glad I went into business for myself. Granted, I've endured some painful losses and challenges along the way, but like the old folks say, God is good all the time.

On August 9, 2002, I launched DMGlobal, the creator of www.Bmorenews, an online journal that covers the black experience in America and beyond, starting in the Baltimore-Washington corridor. The area is home to more than two million African-Americans, and today, Bmorenews.com has firmly stamped its footprint in the region, nationally and internationally. Some of our visitor nations I never knew existed.

I must say the twelve years I've run the business have been simultaneously rewarding, satisfying and humbling. I know I've been afforded opportunities I never imagined, and I love exposing people to things they never knew existed and opening their minds to otherwise unknown possibilities. I call this 'passing it on' because I think as we are blessed we should bless others.

I believe you keep good karma coming your way by doing right by people. The rewards don't necessarily come from where you might think they should, but they come. I've learned one's attitude plays a huge role in one's success. I try to stay sunny and always remain optimistic, no matter how dark things get, because I know the sun will shine again!

Life has a way of humbling everyone, and I'm no exception. Business has taught me some invaluable lessons about life and people, and I've also grown in my faith. I can fully acknowledge God has carried me every step of the way, even when I thought I couldn't go on or when I was dead wrong. My faith teaches me no matter what mistakes we've made, we don't have to repeat them and God's love can more than sustain us. Most importantly, I've learned faith in God has made all the difference in my business. I've found as I keep God in the forefront and center of everything I do, I can do anything except fail.

Hence, I'm therefore compelled to be a blessing to others by sharing my story whenever the opportunity presents itself. I work to give plenty of encouragement to others, especially entrepreneurs, and to remind them they can accomplish anything God tells their spirit to do. I've seen it happen many times. I've seen people go from nowhere to somewhere simply by trusting in God. It happens every day.

A key focus for me is making sure I do my part to empower black people. That's why we aim to present intelligent dialogue on www.bmorenews.com relating to the black experience in the areas of politics, entrepreneurship and business. Even more, I'm a firm believer that parlaying our political power effectively can lead to community economic development. The challenge has been mastering our political leverage and "the ask." You see, many times we get not because we ask not. I'm therefore very interested in us using our power more effectively for our own benefit and development.

I'm of the mindset we in the black community have everything we need to succeed. We simply must learn to work together to better utilize our resources, and we must apply the lessons of the past. For instance, I think given black folk have a trillion dollars in annual disposable income, no black business worth its salt should be struggling. I'm a firm believer when strong black businesses work cooperatively with the church and political leaders, we can create jobs, enabling people to feed their families. Need I say Black Wall Street in Tulsa? What about Black Wall Street in Mound Bayou, Mississippi? For me, this reaches far beyond politics and economics. Simply put, it is spiritual. My faith teaches me black people should not be beggars, regardless of what the other guy does. My faith teaches me when we are faithful, blessings abound like magic and blend into everything we do, say and touch.

I've learned part of having faith is understanding our obligation to bless others as God has blessed us. So I believe you demonstrate the Holy Spirit if you create opportunities for others as you're creating and realizing them for yourself. I'll add there's no greater feeling, for me, than paying people to work for me. There's something in that exchange that feeds my soul and strengthens my self-worth. I've learned it's one thing to create an opportunity for oneself. I've done that. It's another thing, however, to create opportunities for others. Now that's true empowerment! That's how we pass the ball.

From a black perspective, I have to say the more black businesses succeed, the greater the likelihood more black people will become empowered and employed, including those of us with criminal pasts. Given the burgeoning prison industrial complex in America, I'm thoroughly convinced black entrepreneurs and business people are the saving grace for black people in America and beyond. I think at the end of the day, black business owners and black entrepreneurs, the people who have the audacity to try it and win, are the ones most likely to hire blacks who have been imprisoned. The church can certainly be a help, and I think black politicians can play a vital part as well.

Regardless of the challenge, if we can just set our wretched egos aside, we can fix ourselves. Waiting on somebody else to do it for us is not the best use of our time. Instead, we should pull together, get on the same page, form a joint agenda on which the masses can agree and move forward as a race in an otherwise hostile environment. This is our best plan for survival.

If you remember nothing else, always know with God all things are possible regardless of your race, background, mistakes, surroundings, upbringing, family, condition or what happened to you in the past. God allows U-turns. I can attest to that. He allows them for individuals as well as communities and nations.

Black Wall Streets

If God is going to bless Black America, Black America must step up to the plate and step up its game. Ultimately, we must tap back into our greatness as a people. I humbly remind you about Black Wall Street in Tulsa, Okla., which was burned and bombed to the ground by angry whites. Now that might be the finest example of the level of vision I have for Black America today.

Although it was literally destroyed, Black Wall Street in Tulsa developed hundreds of businesses, dozens of churches, restaurants and grocery stores, movie theaters, a half dozen private airplanes, a medical facility, a bank, a post office, schools, libraries, a host of law offices and even a public transportation system. It was founded by O. W. Gurley. Gurley had a grocery store, bought land, and constructed buildings. Ultimately, he and other pioneers attracted blacks from all over and Tulsa eventually became a national symbol of black empowerment.

While Tulsa was by far the most famous, there were also Black Wall Streets across the country in towns like Richmond, Va., Weeksville, N.Y., Baltimore, MD and Durham, N.C. Blacks in business is nothing new to the black community, and that's why I'm so optimistic about our future. I believe in the ultimate possibilities of the universe, and being a student of history only reinforces this belief. Surely if blacks who were once enslaved and those not far removed from slavery can be successful, certainly we can do even more today.

For me, life is about following one's purpose with vigor. I believe my purpose revolves around media, business, politics and service to mankind. Sure there will be some challenges and bumps in the road. Yet I've learned you may get knocked down a million times in life, but if you have the audacity to get up a million and one times that makes you a winner! So, the truth of the matter is everybody can do something special and help make Black America better. Everybody, including children, can play a role in growing the family business. Although there will be difficulties, the black community has incredible potential for growth and progress. But strong leaders who are proud of their blackness must lead the way.

In short, I've learned if you think it, you can do it. If you believe in your heart you can do something, you can. On the other hand, if you believe you can't, you won't. Along these lines, there's absolutely no doubt in my mind as to what the black community can accomplish. We have grown successful businesses in the past and we can do it again. Further, we have always been ingenious and had a propensity for efficiency; it is not new, but innate; just look at our inventions alone, from the fountain pen to dry cleaning.

I should add while entrepreneurship isn't for everyone, it *is* for some. Increasingly, more and more African-Americans are taking that leap of faith and opening the doors to new boutiques or new consulting services. We're often the last ones hired and the first ones fired. So many African-Americans have opted to start their own businesses

Mind you, the entrepreneur is a special breed who understands the hustle, grit and all-nighters entrepreneurship demands. He or she understands working three consecutive days with little or no sleep. An entrepreneur gladly sacrifices for the success of the venture, knows how to turn a "no" into a "know" and hungers success more than sleep, food or water.

I always remind myself God has given me everything I need to succeed. I can work a computer. I can write and tell a story. I can count. The rest is planning, execution and surrounding myself with talented and supportive people.

For a black man in America, nothing can be more liberating than doing for self. People from other races come here, barely able to speak English, and successfully do business – in the black community no less. These merchants, often from South Korea, Pakistan, Nigeria or India, succeed because they have a plan, a support system and finances in place. I maintain black people can do the same thing. Even though I may not have the most money or the best resources, I still believe I can succeed. I think I have what it takes to succeed, and I enjoy being around others who likewise believe in themselves. That which I don't have, I can acquire because I'm willing to do the work, put in the hours, ask relevant questions and accept help in areas where I'm deficient. I'm willing to listen, take classes and attend workshops. I have the wherewithal to do this. And if I play to my strengths, I believe I can do really well and make a nice living in the process with which to take care of myself, my nineteen-year-old son Asaan Payton Glover, and my fourteen-year-old daughter, N'yinde Amaari Glover.

Added to this thirst for a successful business is the fact that I love what I do. I understand the sacrifices, blood, sweat and tears that are required to win. I'm willing to go farther than the next guy, to work longer hours and to deny myself things I want to reach my goal. I know I was born for this. Entrepreneurship runs deep in my veins. Maybe it runs in yours, too?

Chapter 8
The Mission

I embarked on this entrepreneurial journey in August 2002, intent on communicating the black experience to the world and providing the little guy affordable multimedia access. Hence, my business' name is DMGlobal Marketing and Public Relations. Having done graduate work in international affairs, my scope has always been worldwide.

Further, my mission has always been to build a communications network that informs, inspires, and helps improve the conditions of black people around the globe, beginning in my backyard. Why communications? For one, it called me early in life. Also, I've learned the first thing that happens after a takeover is manning the lines of communication.

From East Baltimore to East Africa, from the Middle East to the East Wing of the White House, my overall aim has been to use my skill set to help make life better for my people by providing solid, empowering information about business development, homeownership and employment opportunities. My vision is to better connect the dots, i.e. the elements of the African Diaspora, including Africa, Europe, the Caribbean and the Americas. I would love to see the people in the Diaspora united for the sake of economic cooperation and for relative progress – needed to foster a better quality of life, particularly for the poor and disenfranchised people of color worldwide.

If you ask me, white supremacy has stymied black progress internationally for the past 500 years. Mine is the story of one man's efforts to make a difference, to give back instead of take, to enlighten instead of oppress.

My interest, amidst a world of mainstream media that tends to dominate the psyche of modern man, is to accurately tell the black man's story while pushing an unapologetically black agenda. I want to use media to help empower my community because I have the audacity to believe the story of black people in America is important and must be told. I also believe if I don't write the story, someone of another race will write it and give, at best, a second-hand take on what it means to be black in these United States. Indeed, we're more than what's portrayed in rap videos.

When I questioned my dad early in life about racism, he told me a good way to combat it is to focus on doing what only a black man can do. And so, I fearlessly tell our story to the best of my ability – never resting on yesterday's laurels. I'm personally and passionately committed to black progress. And I try to inspire others to feel the same way.

From communication comes information, and hopefully that helps someone see the larger picture. Our hope is to connect with like-minded people who love Africa and Africans and believe in collaborating to make the journey a little easier and progress a tad quicker. My goal is to effectively communicate to black people and others that despite our condition worldwide, something greater is possible. We are victors, not victims. We are overcomers. We just have to recognize the larger picture and cooperatively commit to doing the necessary work to get to the next level. The key is a spirit of cooperation and belief in ourselves both individually and collectively. We have to believe.

I met a young West African student at Morgan State who told me Africa will never get its act together, much as my father said some thirty years ago. I heard the same about Black America but don't subscribe to that. Instead, I believe in infinite possibilities. Needless to say, this is one key issue on which my father and I disagreed. I do think Africa can turn things around. Similarly, I believe black people worldwide can empower themselves and better determine their own destinies.

I believe black people can work together globally, just like I advocated in my graduate research on Botswana. I know, for example, economic cooperation between Africans and African-Americans is possible because I've been a part of it. Further, I've come to know others, like author extraordinaire Robert Wallace, who love doing business internationally.

Lately, Wallace has been particularly focused on green energy job creation in the states and in Africa. To me, Baltimore Police Top Cop Ed Fox is another African-American entrepreneur who loves doing business internationally. The former Green Beret formed his own trade firm and has been doing business in China full-time for the past several years.

Both men, who I know from living and doing business in Baltimore, demonstrate daily that global African-American economic cooperation is possible and happening as we speak. Long before meeting them, I met Ronald Shakir, who as an Imam had traveled to nearly 100 countries. These three men prove the only limitations are the ones we put on ourselves.

Because of them, I know I can be a player on the world scene. And thanks to people like Dr. Patricia Newton and Frazier Mathis, I've had the opportunity to meet and work with a number of Africans from across the continent.

My business focus at DMGlobal and BMORENEWS.com is to use our skill set to further facilitate black economic cooperation at home and abroad via our own uniquely and organically branded multimedia platform. Understand that I see business as the staple necessary for any community to move forward. Like Marcus Mosiah Garvey, I believe in 'doing for self.' People like Rev. Dr. Leon H. Sullivan demonstrated to us that we do not have to be beggars sitting on bags of gold. We can, in fact, be the owners and the manufacturers. It can be done, indeed!

Dr. Sullivan's African/African-American summits in Harare, Zimbabwe, have been a great motivational force for me because despite the challenges, despite the critics and despite the fact that it had never been done, he consistently pulled together people from across the Diaspora for the sake of developing economic cooperation.

So our aim at DMGlobal is to keep this conversation and continuum going. I'd love to see, for example, the international trade conversation expanded with respect to the U.S. and Africa. I believe there are countless possibilities awaiting those who are seriously interested in African economic cooperation, especially for African-Americans, the Modern Day Josephs. As the adage goes, 'If people knew better, they'd do better.' Many of us go into business stateside, but going into business internationally is also a viable option for those who are committed and prepared.

In the future, I foresee increasingly more people of color engaging in international trade, making deals, doing familiarization tours and learning how to grow business on a global level. That's why it's also important to ensure future generations embrace this entrepreneurial, do-for-self model. Thus, any time Morgan State political science students call on me, I'm there. I want them to know there are older people care about them and what they accomplish. I want to inspire them with ideas the way my professors inspired me. I implore them to think outside the box because mediocrity has its limitations. So why not go for the gold?

I will keep telling this story and planting seeds about economic cooperation while keeping information flowing about the black man's involvement in business ventures worldwide. Of course, it all starts at home, in Baltimore, Washington, D.C., Wilmington, Del., Brooklyn, N.Y., Harlem, N.Y., Philadelphia and Atlanta. For now, the east coast is our main battleground. The strategy is to start in the metropolitan areas closest to home and then expand.

All the while, www.Bmorenews.com affords me to simultaneously touch two hundred nations monthly. That's pretty powerful in terms of influencing people to take positive action. In over a decade of running an Internet-based media and PR outlet, the ever-emerging power of the web has been constantly reiterated and reinforced in my mind as I've seen its power up close and personal.

I've seen the Internet, for example, level the playing field for aspiring media entrepreneurs like myself. Considering everything, I know this is exactly for what I've been called. I also know Tony Brown was spot on in nineteen ninety-three and called it correctly for sure! Today, we can touch thousands with one stroke of a mouse. Just ask the Middle East and North Africa. Their most recent summer of revolution was propelled and fueled immensely by social media like Twitter and YouTube.

Through social media, I aim to keep telling the story of black success and celebrating people like the late corporate takeover guru Reginald F. Lewis, Dr. Ben Carson and Eddie Brown of Brown Capital Management, the second oldest black investment firm in the nation. All three men made history, and Baltimore City is an integral part of their stories.

They and others have been able to make great strides in their respective fields, in part because somewhere along the line they believed they could. Somewhere along the line, something in the water or in the air in Baltimore spoke limitless heights and infinite possibilities to them.

Something got in their heads and had made them think of incredible accomplishments. Sure, there will always be obstacles; however, just like Baltimore attracted blacks from around the country a hundred years ago, giving us the largest number of free blacks in the country, I believe Baltimore still serves as a breeding ground for black empowerment.

When I hear of the works of people like James Jackson and his noted apprentice Isaac Myers, who helped black caulkers in the early 1800's, I'm encouraged by knowing blacks have been doing the damn thing all along in Baltimore. Even while slavery was in play, blacks were nonetheless making strides.

Black America can also entertain like no other, but we're far more than good singers and dancers. We're also world-class surgeons and doctors and engineers. Sure, we can preach with the best of them, but we can also devise unprecedented surgical techniques, help craft historic Civil Rights documents, invent street lights and gas masks, improve the quality of the U.S. Supreme Court and subsequently influence legal decisions around the world.

Why is this history important to me? When I pan the landscape of Black America, I despise the imagery of black people in the media. I vehemently rebuke mainstream media imagery as substandard because it tells only part of the story and too often just the ugly part. I'm sick of the negative stigmatizations and stereotypes that so often brand Black America as 'the bottom of the barrel', the back of the line and the first one out. I don't like seeing young black faces on TV when it comes to news about illegal drugs, as if selling and using drugs is all young blacks do and young whites never commit such crimes. Such poor imagery depicts Black America unfairly, intensifying my goal to provide a more accurate and definitely more inspiring view of my community.

My preference is images of conscientiously strong, masculine black men and intelligent and spiritually rooted black women. Watching mainstream media often feels like watching *"Birth of a Nation".* As black media professionals, our job is to present the most precise image of Black America. We have a lot more pride and greatness than what is promulgated, and it should be illuminated so more people will know the true beauty of black people. When I spoke with Jordanian youth in September 2002 in Amman, they knew nothing about Black history; I learned that much of the world only knows Black America via rap videos; and that's just not good enough for me because my people are so much more than that. Let me also add that I am so proud of artists like Mos Def and 50 Cent who have taken an interest in Africa. Michael Jackson took an interest in Africa, too. Such goodwill deeds improve our international image and I love it.

Correctly telling the story of Black America is as essential to me as breathing air because the young black males accused of dealing drugs typically don't have boats, jets, or connections at U.S. Customs – all of which help keep the cocaine and other drugs flowing to black communities. Of course, that's not to excuse them for using or selling drugs but instead to say that technically they're mere pawns in a much bigger game. The real criminals are on Wall Street, a truth nobody wants to publicly discuss. HBO's *"The Wire"*, based on street life in Baltimore, at least drew attention to the inner-workings of the drug trade. The "real wire" would lead to corporate suites and judicial chambers of some of this nation's most prominent families. The "real wire", according to Chief Fox, is believed to be linked to Wall Street.

I also don't like it that black males comprise forty-four percent of the U.S. prison population, especially when blacks comprise only thirteen point six percent of the U.S. population and when black women, the backbone of the black community, are the fastest growing demographic in prison. This is horribly disproportionate, just like the number of black abortions in America. And seemingly nobody says a peep as if it is normal or to be expected. In any other community, such would be deemed a national emergency.

These facts bother me to no end because something is fundamentally wrong. Not only is this evidence of the disproportionate number of blacks in prison compared to their white counterparts, but it also speaks to the broader plight of blacks in America and the subsequent devastation that such mass incarceration has had and continues to have on families. In a nutshell, America is a hostile territory for blacks, and the prisons are a key component to the strategy to keep blacks marginalized in every way possible.

I also vehemently dislike statistics from Planned Parenthood and others that say black women get four times the number of abortions as white women. While white women get thirty-six percent of the abortions; black women get thirty percent. But again, black people comprise only thirteen point six percent of the US population. For our women to have more abortions, statistically speaking than white women, is startling.

Further, data shows that seventy-eight percent of the abortion clinics are located in black communities. Usually when the issue of abortion is addressed, it's done by right-wingers. After examining the statistics, we should have a problem with the preponderance of abortion clinics in the black community. If you ask me, it should be a topic of Congressional magnitude because it's nothing less than genocide.

For blacks, who are typically Democrats, questioning issues like abortion is taboo. I have a problem with this. One is automatically labeled a trouble maker or confused with being a Republican sympathizer if one raises pertinent questions about abortion – rather than being credited for asking valid questions. My daddy said that I *have* to be able to ask the tough questions.

It's amazing to learn what goes on in the minds of men and women. I, like many other blacks, realize Malcolm X was on point when he noted how both major parties are troublesome for black, and we should have a party solely focused on black issues. I couldn't agree more. And at the very least, we must learn how to use the major parties to our benefit as we did by electing the Ehrlich-Steele ticket in Maryland back in two thousand two.

The first Republican governor in Maryland in thirty-six years, Gov. Robert Ehrlich's victory translated into a lot of progress for a lot of blacks, especially those in business for themselves. Many of us think blacks fared better because Ehrlich had to appease blacks, which he did. The challenge is that ordinarily, the administration in Maryland is majority Democrat. And the Democrats typically have ignored blacks except around election time.

My thought is blacks must learn how to better leverage the black vote to ensure we don't remain marginalized politically, socially or economically. Sure, some escape plight, poverty and devastation to family, however, many don't. Given blacks are thirty percent of Maryland's population, I think we deserve a lot more than Democrats give.

Hence, our underlying mission at DMGlobal and Bmorenews is the empowerment of our community, because blacks are just as important as anybody else in America. This isn't about complaining but instead calling a spade a spade. Too often, even blacks think the black community is undeserving. But I believe nothing could be farther from the truth.

A black woman once told me it's a white man's world, and I've never heard anything more absurd in my life. I don't think it's accurate in the least. What disturbed me about her comment was its origin: years of neglect and abuse. Too many blacks have a defeatist attitude as did she, but my faith teaches me this is God's world and therefore belongs to everybody.

While the "white man", or the Global North, is very influential in this day and time, I know I'm just as much a part of God's green earth as anybody else. So, I disagree with the mindset of limitations and replace it with a mindset of possibilities. I choose to view life from a different perspective in that I'm a citizen of the universe and refuse to be bound by the limited thinking of others. I also refute anybody thinking for me. I can think for myself, and, my hope is we do a better job of thinking for ourselves.

The world belongs to whoever goes out and seizes opportunities. As they say, the early bird gets the worm. Nobody has a monopoly on knowledge. So, just like white, Asian or Latino men, I can go out there and succeed, too.

It's true the Global North has control of much of the world's economic system. However, I also know the Global South is from where oil and many other natural resources are generated.

Further, if it's the white man's world, why are parts of the European economy performing so poorly, even with their many neo-colonialist ties to Global South nations? I'm no economist, but that tells me somebody is doing something wrong.

Too often, people speculate about things for which they have no clue, and inaccurate information causes financial disruptions. Even worse, greed and selfishness leave countries, like too many in Africa, poor and destitute – even countries that have natural resources with which to supply the world.

The truth is nobody knows how a given economy will react to market forces, especially one with a culture of reckless spending. When you spend more than you make, you've got problems. And problems will continue until spending on frivolous, non-productive things is replaced by investing in the betterment of society. And you know, there are so many layers to the world market it just makes sense for nations to work together.

I think free trade wouldn't be a problem if it weren't for greed. Sadly, I believe the greed of a few makes life miserable for the masses. Helping others is a core value for me, in part, because I think we can all do more to help each other. Likewise, racism and classism prevent fundamental assistance from reaching those who need it most. In many instances, people of the same race impede each other. I just wish we could see beyond skin color, class or tribe and see each other as human beings.

Of course, that's not how capitalism works. Its premise is competition and free market trade with little room for humanity. The basis of capitalism, in its raw, Wall Street form, is sink or swim, and that's where politics and media come into play because they both nurture the insatiable beast. I think, as a result, capitalism has heavily co-opted our traditional family values.

Today, TVs are rearing children and traditional values have flown out the window as society is more focused on perception than reality. The values instilled in us by our grandparents and great-grandparents seem a distant memory. Children have little respect for their elders, and they're in jeopardy of losing what they do have because of what they pick up from TV, video games and some rap music.

I want to see a world where blacks are producing and manufacturing and growing viable enterprises just as whites and many in European nations do. I think the more images blacks see of other blacks making progress, the better off blacks will be and the more likely we'll begin accomplishing economic parity nationally and internationally.

This is why I envision building a television network that reaches across the world, particularly to Africa. This is my dream. Another one of my dreams, believe it or not, is becoming President of the United States of Africa. Yep, I said it. Why not?

I want to provide educational programming featuring history and culture to enable blacks throughout the Diaspora to learn about good, positive happenings in black communities around the world. A public television network would be nice, but the Internet is working just fine for now. Of course, we'd need buy-in from our strategic partners. Again, I would start with countries who want to be a part of this and go from there. Call me an eternal optimist, but I truly believe it can happen.

We can't look to mainstream media to produce programming and news segments that instill pride in black folk. And you know, it's not somebody else's job to inspire me and mine. That's my task. It may be difficult, but I sure plan to try. Worldwide, the black family is under attack. I believe we have it rougher than any other race, so if I can add some culturally enriching information and material to the conversation, more people will be enlightened.

The global system of white supremacy makes it difficult for most blacks. Certainly, some blacks are proactive and get assistance from sincere non-blacks. I've seen it in Ethiopia, West Baltimore, New York City, Canada, Jamaica and Tanzania. However, blacks in the Diaspora are too often inundated with weak images of blacks in subservient roles, including butlers and maids. I have a problem with such imagery and despise the mindset that considers a black man worthy only of being a butler versus a general or a president, like Toussaint L'Overture, the most powerful black man of his time. From the Middle East to Southeast D.C., the media images of blacks portray people who don't possess positive values like going to college and being part of functional, loving families. Instead, we're portrayed as shiftless people content to live off the government.

My goal is to battle the negative stigmas and present black success stories. I want people to be aware of the social challenges facing blacks, i.e. poverty, illegal drugs, over-incarceration, over-abortion, under-education and the proliferation of guns. But I also want people to know about the good, wholesome things blacks are doing despite those challenges. Successful black business stories are my favorite, especially when the entrepreneur has a spiritually uplifting testimony. I really love sinking my teeth into such stories.

When people mutually respect each other, they work together better. That's why my work is in Africa as well as in America. Africans have had to deal with colonialism and neo-colonialism by European powers. When you look at South Africa, for instance, you see that despite it being home to some of the largest diamond reserves in the world, many of its black people live in deplorable conditions. Education and communication, I believe, are essential to eliminating that disparity. A pen pal of mine in Pretoria, Mell Sibeko, sends me encouragement all the time; and I send it right back.

Similarly, in the United State it's painfully obvious blacks have been targeted by the powers-that-be since slavery ended.

The so-called "Negro Dilemma," or what to do with four million freed ex-slaves, explains why being black in America is perpetually burdensome. First we were sold into slavery, and then we were freed and eventually allowed to integrate mainstream America. Many white people oppose black progress. Has that changed some? Yes. But it sure as hell hasn't happened quickly enough, and racism is still just as insidious today as it was in nineteen sixty-four when historic Civil Rights legislation was passed.

From Africa to the slave ship to America, the black man has been on a long perilous journey: the Ma'afa. Personally, I'd like to see blacks in America, as well as our brethren in Africa, get our just due. I'd like to see the black man prosper – everywhere.

I think the black man's rightful place in the world has been twisted. While he once gave Europe the arts and sciences, he is currently failing at world politics. Too often, others have benefited from his labor and his resources in Africa and in America. This is why media is so important to me. I believe the more the black man comes to see himself in his proper light, the more likely he is to respect himself and see himself in a more meaningful role internationally – manufacturer versus consumer, boss versus employee. When our mindsets change, our circumstances change and we begin to gain much-needed respect. I happen to think black media can help adjust our focus, perception and self-definition, as proven repeatedly by film producer Spike Lee.

Black folk must return to the values laid out by the ancestors and elders. My grandparents taught me to respect and honor God, to be well-learned, have manners, and to be a better person. I think 'common sense' was their term. They understood all of the education in the world can't replace it.

Quite often the challenge doesn't lie only in how the black man views himself. White supremacy is deeply entrenched in the annals of this nation and Europe. Foreigners coming to America for the very first time often have preconceived negative notions of African-Americans as second-class citizens. I have a problem with that. My ancestors died for this country. Therefore, this land is my land and you *will* respect me.

It's as if foreigners come here with a mindset that blacks are the permanent underclass and, as a result, don't deserve the best products or quality service. Sadly, until others get to know us for themselves, they will continue perpetuating false stereotypes and prejudices about us. As a journalist and a media person, I must report these challenges to the world in hopes of effecting positive change.

The more we understand issues, the better our chances of devising viable solutions to them. You see, light and darkness can't dwell in the same place at the same time, so I choose the light.

Clearly the U.S. was perplexed with what to do with four million freed blacks, so numerous remedies were put forth. Along the way, unspeakable hate and violence erupted toward blacks, racist acts that persist to some extent today.

Progress is being made, but it's not enough. Having a black president forty-five minutes down the road gives way to optimism, but the harsh reality is black folk still get the shaft in this country. The black community is still under attack overtly by Republicans and covertly by Democrats. Comparatively, though, blacks in the U.S. enjoy a better standard of living than most blacks anywhere else in the Diaspora – even when you consider there are many African nations with kings, queens, princes, princesses and others who live like royalty.

African nations have many challenges, including corruption, coup d'états, blood diamonds, neo-colonial powers like De Beers, a cartel of companies that dominate the diamond industry, HIV/AIDS, underdevelopment, under-education, famine and subpar medical care. Helping Africa is categorically a non-factor from a Western perspective. A good example is how the U.S. stood idly by while the genocide portrayed in "Hotel Rwanda," starring actor Don Cheadle, occurred. But neither the European countries nor the United States have any problem mining for natural resources in Africans' backyards.

This is why I excitedly get out of bed and rush to my computer each morning. I know there's no telling what story might come across my desk. From West Africa to West Baltimore, every single day is different. After all, I cover the gamut. The overarching concept of my message, however, is the empowerment of my community.

I love when a story is positive, but if it *is* negative that presents an opportunity for me to give my unique Afrocentric perspective. For instance, here's a startling example of something I've learned of late that is compelling, provocative and all the while devastating, yet is sparking no national outrage. To be truthful, I was disgusted over only recently finding out about this because it has been going on since slavery ended. I'm talking about the eugenics movement, in which since nineteen seventy-three some sixteen million black babies have been aborted in the United States.

Considering there are thirty-six million blacks in the country, this means we have lost over half of our race's numbers because of the racist philosophy of the eugenicists who legalized abortion, the pill, hysterectomies and sterilization and then pushed them on the black community like they were going out of style. Where is the outrage?

Interesting and sadly, in July 2013, North Carolina Gov. Pat McCrory signed into law a ten million dollar compensation package to be distributed among living victims of the state's eugenics practices. The move by McCrory followed a ten-year deliberation process and is to make amends for the estimated seven thousand six hundred people the state sterilized by choice, force or coercion under the authority of the North Carolina Eugenics Board program between 1929 and 1974. Verified victims will be issued a share of the ten million dollars by two thousand fifteen.

The aim all along by these elite whites like Planned Parenthood Founder Margaret Sanger has been to exterminate black people. The elitists might prefer the term population control. Don't believe me?

In my opinion, Planned Parenthood has targeted blacks from the onset, along with Latinos. Consider this: Planned

Parenthood is so insidious that it went beyond the U.S. borders with its population control efforts, developing Planned Parenthood International with a goal to increase abortions in Africa some eighty-two percent by two thousand fifteen. They not only want to kill black babies in the United States; they've now gone to the very source of black people.

Now, they don't view it this way. They say they are helping provide contraception. Some would justify this targeted action, which I view as genocide. Believers in the Malthusian Theory, for instance, insist there are too many people to feed. So, somebody has to get voted off of the island. My problem is the process by which it's determined which folks live and which folks die. What gives them the right to decide other people's fates? These people are not God, and they don't have that right, despite a billion dollar or so annual operating budget.

And so, I attack each day like an Olympic athlete in training, like a Navy SEAL on a covert mission or like a sniper aiming at a target. I deal with complicated topics like abortion and more simplistic issues like employment, but at the end of the day my focus is the Black Diaspora.

My attack mechanisms are emails, Bmorenews posts, weekly radio shows, social media, TV interviews, video interviews, quotes in *The Washington Post*, guest appearances on other people's radio shows and Internet radio shows. I also get invitations to speaking engagements and have spoken at Georgetown University, a church in Arusha, Tanzania, and at the United Nations. Eventually, we hope to expand it to the Midwest and the West Coast.

I cannot omit our regular business networking events called the Black Wall Street Series *NYC *MD *DC *ATL, which features the Joe Manns Black Wall Street Awards. We celebrate black entrepreneurs and professionals as well as the people who support them – regardless of race.

These events and other outreach efforts allow us to put our clients and advertisers in direct communiqué with potential customers and afford attendees an opportunity to grow their networks.

To date, the Black Wall Street Series has been held in Baltimore, Washington D.C., Harlem, N.Y. and Atlanta, after originally being named at the Harambee Dinner Club in 2002. Harambee is Swahili and means "all pull together." Thanks to strategic partnerships with entities like Sisters4Sisters Network, Inc. and the CEO Business Café, we've been able to cover more ground.

Hence, this is my formula, if you will, for continued success: jab, jab, right hook, left hook, overhand right. Knock out! Each week, it's about pulling together and posting news stories and videos on Bmorenews, hosting the WOLB weekly radio show, making TV appearances, disseminating our email newsletter and attending business networking events. Additionally, I constantly meet with entrepreneurs who want exposure. After all, one of my slogans is, "I'll make you famous!"

Our mission at DMGlobal is not to save the world but instead to provide clients with similar media access via text, photos and videos. But be clear that this is a business, not an expensive hobby. Therefore, our primary goal is to make a profit without selling our souls, while advocating on behalf of the underdog in society. You know who the underdog is: It's the black community.

There's no way I could see all of the disparity facing my community and not fight back. But I've learned I can't save everybody or be everybody's hero. I've learned I must have balance in my advocacy efforts.

Nowadays I don't volunteer for everything or to help every cause like I once did. I have to use my resources where I can do the most good. I do a good job of discerning exactly what I can and cannot do. You see, I've found if I'm not careful people will use me up and, when I'm no longer valuable to them or they've gotten what they need from me, I'll be discarded and they'll be on to the next benevolent soul. I've also learned time is money and 'if I'm too busy, I'm too cheap.' At least that's what J. D. Howard, Baltimore's internationally renowned photographer, says. Again, I can't spend time on every cause, but I do my small part to inform, inspire and help improve other's lots in life. Again, the goal is to be profitable, so it's a constant balancing act. I want to give, but I do not want to be abused. Even more, I have to make time to be a good dad – something I cannot reiterate enough.

I've also learned if you don't know your value, other people will assign a value to you, which far too often means less profit. And I can't have that. I've learned if I'm not driving, somebody else is. I've learned in most any situation, there is somebody who's making things happen and somebody to which things are happening. Therefore, it is imperative my time is used wisely and that I work from a position of power. Minorities in

America often get the short end of the stick. Instead of manufacturing, we are consuming. Instead of leading, we are following. I believe in a more self-determined approach to life whereby one takes charge of the situation.

That is the nature of capitalism and free market enterprise: to expand one's control and grasp of an industry or market. Therefore, to survive in America you have to understand the system and how it works. You have to understand how to create a niche based on your own unique skill set, gifts and talents. Play to your strengths. And then, with every ounce of power you can muster, go out and apply yourself to the task at hand. Every single day for the past twelve years, DMGlobal has been my reason for living – along with, of course, my children and my family.

"Know your value" is a phrase my adopted mom says often and one I repeat all the time. For me, knowing my value means knowing what my services are worth. As an African-American media entrepreneur, I've learned so many lessons. I've learned to always be open to negotiation and to assess if a given situation is likely to be a good fit or a bad fit. Negotiations signal forward progress but require effective communication. Closing the deal is a very important skill not possessed by everyone, which is why listening is so very critical. Knowing when and how to act is vital.

So my life involves helping others through my business and ensuring I charge appropriate fees. One of the greatest investments for me, besides mentoring, is educating small business owners about what I can do for their businesses.

Quite often, I run into small business owners who don't understand the necessity of marketing, so I have to explain the process to them.

Many small business owners are apprehensive about paying for marketing, primarily because they really don't understand how it all works together. So when times are tight, the marketing budget is the first thing to get cut. Personally, I don't think we should ever stop marketing ourselves because there are always affordable ways of getting the word out. Providing affordable marketing tools for businesses is what I do. And I absolutely love it!

It took me two years to convince one client in particular that hiring Bmorenews could be good for his business. After that point, he became my absolute best customer for four years. The lesson I learned was that sometimes I'd have to work a tad harder to educate people about the benefits of web advertising. I learned all fruit was not low-hanging, and convincing some new clients may take some effort. But it can be done.

No matter how much time I invest in explaining our benefits to potential clients, some people just don't get it. The Internet is the newest kid on the block in terms of advertising, so, it takes time for people to get on board. In any event, one must learn how to balance it all out.

Others do get it, though. Take Marcel Umphery, the wiz kid of home mortgages. Featured in the October 2012 edition of *Black Enterprise*, he's a regular client because he understands one thing: Once his press release hits Bmorenews.com, his

"Google-ability" immediately and tremendously improves. Others know this as well, including our visitors from around the world. Every night, I review what people are searching on Bmorenews so I'll have a greater understanding of what they're interested in and what gets the most attention – valuable information that allows me to better serve my followers across all platforms.

Of course, a key first step is determining whether a potential client is a good fit. How much time is required to prime the client? Can he or she cover my fees? Is this a good investment of my time and effort? It's critical for me to decide these answers in as short a time as possible because time is money and I loathe wasting time.

On the other hand, I knew early on that eighty percent of my business would come from repeat customers, as conventional wisdom suggests. I've interacted with thousands of entrepreneurs from around the world and know some people are just not worth the effort. But by the same token, I've had some wonderful clients bless me in wonderful ways I couldn't imagine.

Oftentimes my small business owners need a lot of time and attention at the outset of a project, especially if they're launching a massive campaign. Often, these clients have great needs but lack the resources to pay for the necessary marketing. Counter to that, I've had some well-off clients who I bill a grand a month though they require my services for only twenty minutes a month. These are dream clients whose checks, which I don't have to worry about bouncing, mind you, help offset the nominal amounts other clients struggle to pay.

By the way, in twelve years of business, I've had only a handful of checks to bounce. The point is whether clients have a lot or a little, they still deserve my absolute best service. And it is my job, if I take on the client, to deliver just that. After all, if there are no customers, there is no business. So, we have to take great care of all of our clients – the ones paying a thousand a month as well as the ones paying three hundred dollars a month. One is no less important than the other.

An entrepreneur, like an Olympian, understands he or she will run into obstacles seen and unseen. There will be a lot of "no's" and plenty of mistakes. Yet, the successful entrepreneur, I have found, learns to turn lessons learned into nuggets of wisdom and fertilizer for future success. Entrepreneurship is a journey I'm glad I began a long time ago when I was serving newspapers all over West Baltimore. I'm certain I could never again work a nine-to-five job as I've been an entrepreneur in some form or fashion for most of my life. Entrepreneurship stretches and tests my faith and abilities, but it's what I do.

I may or may not get rich, but I'm definitely living a purpose-filled life, a life my parents would be immeasurably proud of. I get to determine when I work and what jobs I work. I punch no clocks, and no one's breathing down my neck or sweating me. I realized a long time ago I can make more money working for myself than I can working for someone else. Not everyone supported my decision at the time, but I persevered nonetheless.

Further, given the beginning years of this business are rooted in the worst economy since 1929, a powerful black investment banker told me it's a miracle I've survived so long.

If I can hold on, I'm sure a brighter economy is on the horizon. I believe my new contacts from yesterday will mature into profitable contracts tomorrow. I believe if I stick to my routine and tweak it when and where necessary, things will get easier soon. I just have to remember that business has its cycles and those who best adjust to changing times are the most likely to succeed.

As it relates to the broader scope of DMGlobal, particularly the media aspect, the goal has always been to report on the status and condition of black people worldwide from an Afrocentric perspective. My mega-dream is to own an international television network, just like the Seventh Day Adventists have. I got a chance to "enjoy" their network while I was in Tanzania, as it was the only media to which I had access. In any event, I absolutely love what I do: telling the story of my people through my own eyes.

And that's a taste of a walk in my shoes: corporate sponsorship lunches, evening fundraisers for local and state politicians in the DMV area and breaking stories on behalf of the minority business or the disabled veterans' business enterprise community.

Honestly, I sometimes feel like a fireman because it seems every time I turn around there's a new fire for me to extinguish. You see, while my business markets companies and individuals, my job entails much more than running ads for them. Truthfully, I never know what people are going to ask of me. For instance, I once got a phone call about a person's granddaughter being arrested and getting no bail, and I even once received a call about a fire on the seventeenth floor of the senior citizens building in Sandtown, no matter that I was emceeing an event with R&B singer Mario and Baltimore NBA star Carmelo Anthony in Owings Mills at the time.

Truthfully, with my business there is never a dull moment. I might get a call from a fellow entrepreneur who is struggling and needs a moment of prayer and encouragement, or a call about discrimination. People call me about racism, lynchings, illegal arrests, murders, firings, evictions, false charges, extortion and political corruption including the misappropriation of campaign funds or the use of bogus addresses for candidates. Through it all, I strive to give God all of the glory.

In my business, I get to see the black experience on all levels. And yes, that includes from the prisons. I've been contacted by a man seeking freedom after being locked up for thirty years, asked to investigate a local politician and to do an expose on governmental agency corruption. No question, no two days – or no two elections – are the same.

For more than a decade, this is what I've done. Political candidates call me. Incumbents who want to get re-elected call me. People from both sides of the aisle call me, too, and that's a good thing because I've found the line in the Democratic Party has a lot of people ahead of me. On the Republican side, however, there's a shorter line and a bigger and faster pay day. Both have their strengths and both have their flaws. My thought is you have to roll with whatever comes your way, give it your best shot and then move on to the next assignment.

I *will* say this: I've made more money in a month with a Republican than I've made in several years with a Democrat. And that's being polite. I've found that in general, Democrats often lack an understanding of the entrepreneurial model and they don't fully understand business or relationships. From a social-issues standpoint, Democrats look out for the masses better. If you doubt that last statement, just remember the response President Barack Obama gave New Jersey residents after Hurricane Sandy, versus the response President George Bush gave New Orleans residents after Hurricane Katrina.

Actor Mike Myers looked at rapper Kanye West as though he was crazy when West went off script during a nationally televised program to raise money for Hurricane Katrina victims and said, "George Bush doesn't care about black people." But when you consider the demographics of New Orleans and the egregiously slow response time from the government to that devastating, Category Five storm that took at least a thousand lives, what other conclusion can you draw?

I must insert that politics is in on three levels: local, national, and international. Thus, I think we have to remember that it is all relative. A Republican from Maryland may not be like a Republican from Texas; similarly, a Democrat representing Massachusetts may be the complete opposite of another Democrat from the same state. My point is that we have to judge the merits of each situation on a case by case basis. We cannot afford to give *anybody* a free pass, regardless of race or party. At the end of the day, all I want to know is how well you are treating my people. That's it!

I've learned how to do business with people of both major parties. I'm sure that I dare to conduct business with Republicans is considered blasphemous by some, but nothing could be more ignorant. If you're in business, all people are potential customers, whether they're Democrats or Republicans, black or white or straight or gay. I don't subscribe to such chicanery when it comes to party politics. Further, I find Republicans can be extremely helpful on issues affecting black people, especially on the state level as was the case of Maryland Lt. Gov. Michael S. Steele.

In my opinion, over the past decade no other black elected official in Maryland, besides Rep. Elijah Cummings, has spoken up more for black people than Michael Steele. At the same time, I will do business with Democrats if they get themselves together. The disingenuous part about Democrats, to me, is the white males in the party think blacks are stupid. Or, at least, that's how it appears. They don't seem to value our intellect, and quite often they'll tout buzzwords and terms like 'minority business enterprise' (MBE) or 'new school construction', yet at the end of the day we see the same dismissal of the black community that always happens. To be fair, Maryland's MBE program is a national model with a twenty-nine percent MBE participation goal; however, blacks get only a very small percentage of those set asides. This is unacceptable. Further, I know if I don't make noise about black business and MBE to our elected officials, set asides will disappear.

Arnold M. Jolivet, a leading MBE proponent who recently passed – along with D.C. Mayor for Life Marion Barry – said a

Mass Transit Administration project in Maryland lowered the MBE goal from twenty-five percent to seven percent. Given that blacks comprise thirty percent of the state's population, this is unacceptable. If you ask me, the State of Maryland still has a lot of making up to do for years of blatant neglect to minority businesses and the minority community, overall. Unfortunately, the vestiges of slavery remain in the minds of some still-backwards people who are both white *and* black.

I've found that too often our black representatives lack the cohesiveness and resolve to stand for something in Annapolis and in D.C. Former state Senator Clarence Mitchell, III, also known as C3 or The Bear, told me that back in the seventies when he was in office, there were only eleven blacks in the Maryland General Assembly. Former State Senator Tommie Broadwater, the first black state senator from Prince George's County, made the same observation: he said they got more accomplished in his day with fewer people. Today, however, there are four times as many officials in the state capital working on behalf of blacks. The question is whether they are four times as powerful. "Bear" said they're not up to snuff and were not bringing back the type of legislative victories synonymous to their numbers. C3 passed along with Joviet and Barry while I was writing this book, but I'm reminded just how strong an effective black leader can be. This is particularly poignant at a time when many black elected officials seem to have abandoned the struggle for black parity in America. It's almost as if racism and discrimination in America are dead issues and the days of real black politicians who speak up for black people are a thing of the past, which I think is nothing less than awful.

In my experience, black Democrats have to fight for attention in Maryland and throughout the country. The only time black Democrats are important to the Democratic Party, from my vantage point, is at voting time. As for a black agenda, that seems nearly impossible at times. The 2012 Democratic National Convention is a classic example. Everybody's lobby was loud, all the way down to the lobby seeking to put "God" and "Jerusalem" back on the platform; however, I did not observe a similar level of noise and activism around a black agenda. I think the black agenda gets dissipated with other special interest groups and, consequently, loses its voice.

Nonetheless, I live, eat and breathe politics – forever gauging a candidate's electability, analyzing black and white political voting trends, such as an increasingly conservative Maryland, and perusing the resumes and backgrounds of potential candidates who are jockeying for statewide and national office.

After all, these are the issues local TV networks want to discuss when they call me. It's my job to know the issues, the players, who has the money, who has the relationships, who has the skeletons and who has the admirable track record of service. Political astuteness is a critical part of what makes Bmorenews and DMGlobal unique from other media and marketing outlets because at the end of the day, my job is to know who wins the next election. On this note, I have successfully predicted the last three governors of Maryland, including the most recent in 2014, Larry Hogan, and his Lieutenant Governor, Boyd K. Rutherford.

Chapter 9
Bmorenews' Specialty
Covering Black Political Economy in the DMV

I learned about the interrelationship of politics and economics in graduate school at Morgan State University, where I majored in international affairs, and the insight I gained was priceless. I was introduced to how the world works and learned it was divided between the Global North and the Global South. This perspective applies both domestically *and* globally. I came to better understand what can happen when, despite an organized Global North, the people of the Global South take a self-empowering, proactive approach to empowerment. I believe nobody is going to do for us what we can and should do for ourselves. Hence, the DMV is rich with success stories from business and political standpoints. In fact, I'd venture to say the black people living in the DMV are some of the most politically astute blacks in America.

Because I'm among only a few black media types in Maryland with the ability to communicate fast and strong via print, radio, TV and the web to thousands stateside and abroad in a moment's notice, I'm what many folks call influential. All of this, of course, is based on timing. As experts through the ages have noted time and again, timing and presentation are everything. Translation: Bmorenews has become a meaningful voice in the DMV. We have been vocal on issues when others were silent. We have given voice to those without one. And we have illuminated what others prefer remains hidden.

Hopefully, these efforts over the years are translating into a more empowered black community.

I think it's critical for blacks to have a voice in the DMV, where there's so much going on and so much money at stake. Politics often help determine who gets the resources, and our aim is to ensure blacks get as much of the pie as possible. To that end, we can't afford to be strangers at City Hall in D.C., at the State House in Annapolis or at City Hall in Baltimore. It's no accident we've visited the Obama White for news coverage over twenty times. The way I see it, the more times the better for black folk!

Politics in the DMV fascinate me, and I absolutely love it! I also have come to know that we must master politics. Hence, I'm incredibly entrenched in the political landscape that I've been able to accurately predict the winners of elections weeks or months in advance. I once called an election spread within two points of the actual Baltimore City mayoral election – on television, no less. This was in 2003, the year local black favorite and high school principal Dr. Andrey Bundley challenged then-Mayor Martin O'Malley, an Irish-American, using a pro-black platform in a majority black city.

This was four years after O'Malley handily beat two black mayoral candidates, Lawrence Bell and Carl Stokes. A noted Jewish PR man said Bundley, who had a growing groundswell of support, wouldn't get twenty percent of the vote. The critic made his bold prediction live on WBAL TV 11, the city's NBC affiliate; I predicted he'd get thirty percent of the vote. Turns out Bundley garnered thirty-two percent of the vote, in a losing effort. Many people later said Bundley got the anti-O'Malley vote. I said it didn't matter, and I was proud to see African-Americans once again politically engaged around a black leader. The last time a black man was celebrated citywide was in the nineties when Mayor Kurt L. Schmoke was in office.

In short, Bmorenews' beat is Black America, beginning with the two million or so black people in the DMV. With the assistance of our strategic partners, our team has also been growing Bmorenews' presence north to New York, west to Chicago and Portland and south to Atlanta. Online, of course, our reach is global.

I consider the DMV a jewel, politically speaking. And since I launched my business, I've tried to include as much D.C. politics in what I give my followers as I can. The way I see it, I can't be relevant in journalism or politically speaking if I don't know my stuff when it comes to D.C. So, person by person I've worked diligently to cultivate and sustain relationships with folk in D.C. and Prince George's (PG) County. Heck, I've also made a friend or two in neighboring Montgomery County, like former Delegate Herman Taylor.

I've been in love with Prince George's County since one of my mentors and colleagues, William Hopson, introduced me to it years ago. He took me to Woodmore Estates, and I immediately felt empowered to see so many well-to-do African-Americans living side-by-side in million dollar homes around a golf course. Now, that's sexy! Of course, I think it's sexy when black folk inhabit $250,000 homes, too. You see, for far too long we've been denied jobs with salaries adequate enough to support home ownership, or sensible loans from reputable mortgage companies that make owning homes affordable. Because of that, many of us have abandoned the dream of home ownership and are content renting apartments and homes. Now I'm not putting renters down. Hell, I was one before I bought my first home. But I just can't overstate how much it warmed my heart to go to Woodmore Estates and learn that the folk living in those nice, big houses with neatly manicured lawns looked just like me.

Being a journalist has opened many doors for me. For one, www.Bmorenews.com has served as a news media resource for people in Prince George's County and D.C., just as it has for Baltimore businesses, politicians, artists and community groups. And our weekly radio show, which began in 1999, has served as a news media resource for D.C. folk just as it has for those in Baltimore. We've had many guests on our show from the Capital Region – like Joe Gaskins, Founder & CEO of the *Prince George's County* Contractors & Business Association - because I believe we have more legitimate reasons to work together than we do to work independently. We share similar issues, so it only makes sense to build bridges between Baltimore and D.C., two majority black Eastern seaboard cities.

Over the years, I've interviewed former D.C. Mayor Marion Barry on several occasions, experiences I credit with helping me thoroughly appreciate the mindset of black Washingtonians. Likewise, interviewing Mayor Barry served as a constant reminder that black people can do just about anything we want – if we apply ourselves.

When I think about what Mayor Barry meant to so many people in the District, I'm honored, humbled and grateful for the time he shared with me. After all, say what you want about him, but the man is an icon. Further, he was so very down to earth and always willing to help a brother out. I thank God for people like him because though he'd risen to some pretty high heights, he remained committed to helping people when he could. You know, oftentimes some of us "make it" and don't even think about trying to help others accomplish their dreams and goals, too. But that was not the case with Mayor Barry. I can attest to the fact that he sincerely helped others, as evidenced by his funeral which was fit for a king.

Barry and the other black mayors of Washington, D.C., are a great reminder of black political empowerment and proof of what can be accomplished in the future when people work together. I've always said that, compared to Baltimore, D.C. really 'gets it' nowadays. After all, they've kept a black mayor for nearly four decades – from Walter Washington in nineteen seventy-five to Muriel Bowser today. That black men and women – let's not forget Sharon Pratt Kelly was mayor from nineteen ninety-one to nineteen ninety-five – have been the top political leaders in the nation's capital since nineteen seventy-five is a powerful testament to the beautiful unity parlayed by African-Americans in the District. I love that, I appreciate that and I very much wish for similar camaraderie in my hometown.

I want to see black political leaders in Baltimore and in Prince George's County stand more united on a collective agenda that is not authored elsewhere, and I want to see self-determined black leadership that is proud to serve a majority black population without fear. In D.C., I get to see what Baltimore could be in certain ways, politically speaking. Clearly, blacks in Baltimore have the ability to be more politically effective. Unfortunately, I think a lot of the past black political will that made Baltimore so meaningful in the Civil Rights struggle has been lost. Truthfully, I think it has been dormant since 1999.

And this is exactly where I want to see black people in Baltimore, D.C. *and* Prince George's resurrect and rebound such that we are indelibly woven into the very fabric of anything moving. With every new hotel, office building, or stadium, I want to see black people in charge and hiring other black people. To me, nothing is more beautiful. Of course, I want to see all people succeed, but I must first start at home.

Travelling between D.C. and Prince George's County has been empowering and profitable and has expanded my circle and sphere of influence. It has also afforded me the opportunity to build new relationships with a brand new demographic of like-minded people. Along the way, I've met some really brilliant minds. I always scout for great news stories, and the Capital Region has a lot of black entrepreneurs and a lot of black politicos. Simply put, it's a gold mine from a news perspective, a political perspective *and* a business perspective. These aspects, I think, make www.Bmorenews.com a "triple threat".

Can I say again how much I just love Prince George's County? It really does my heart good to see a preponderance of upwardly mobile, politically astute African-Americans who are parlaying their political power into economic benefit. But that's Prince George's County, which has long been hailed as the wealthiest black jurisdiction in the country.

Presently, Prince George's County's growing delegation of state senators and state delegates wields greater potential political power in the Maryland General Assembly than ever before. And thanks to redistricting – the redrawing of state district lines, which happens every ten years in conjunction with the U.S. Census – they have more black political capital than blacks in Baltimore. In fact, a consistent trend in the past twenty years has been for Baltimoreans to leave the city with some headed for nearby Prince George's County – making Prince George's County even stronger. Additionally, PG County has more blacks than any of the other twenty-three jurisdictions in Maryland, including Baltimore County, so it's now the new hub of black power in the state. No question.

Clearly, many of these black folks are serious about progress. Although they have astuteness and business savviness, they didn't have a Bmorenews.com. They *do* have, however, WPGC radio station and *The Washington Informer Newspaper.*

The short of it is that I felt there was an opportunity for www.Bmorenews to step in and shine. I can write or video a story and have it out in an hour, a service that at times is priceless. Sure, there are media outlets in Prince George's

County, including some publications; however, we have toiled arduously for the past twelve years to build a bridge with our brethren there via Bmorenews.com. should add that part of my pleasure over the years has been covering dynamic individuals like Wayne Curry, a noted attorney who was the first black County Executive in Prince George's. Now, that was a man who understood that black people needed a bigger piece of the pie. No doubt! A couple of years back, he considered reentering politics and making a run for statewide office, so a member of his team asked www.Bmorenews.com to help get the word out. During the writing of this book, he too passed away.

Curry eventually chose not to run, but the energy in the black community was electric. For instance, hundreds of people showed up for his birthday party that year, proving he still had incredible reach and influence in the county. A lot of people showed great interest in a potential political resurgence by Curry, likely because he shared the mindset of the upwardly mobile blacks in the area.

For me, it was highly demonstrative that the right black candidate at the right time can indeed take the helm in Maryland – especially one who can excite Prince Georgians. Again, they are indeed a force to be respected.

During the writing of this book, we held a Black Wall Street business networking event in Seat Pleasant, located in Prince George's. At the event, a virtual "Who's Who" of Prince George's County politics were present. Besides Tommie Broadwater, other attendees included Judge Alexander Williams, the first black State's Attorney from Prince George's

County and the first black federal judge to represent the Southern District of Prince George's County; Floyd E. Wilson, the first black County Council member elected in the county; former State Senator Nathaniel Exum, the third black State Senator from Prince George's County; Tommie Thompson, the longest-serving Housing Director for Prince George's County; and Sylvester J. Vaughns, the Past President of the NAACP and a participant in the landmark Supreme Court decision to integrate the Prince George's County School System (Vaughns v. Board of Education). To say the least, I gained an even deeper appreciation for blacks in Prince George's County after attending this event. By working with like-minded individuals in the county like Seat Pleasant Mayor Eugene Grant and politico extraordinaire Dr. Wilbert Wilson, we have grown our reach in the wealthiest black jurisdiction in the nation even more.

Anyway, as J.D. Howard always says, "You can't teach what you don't know, and you can't rule where you don't go." When it's all said and done, the time I invested growing our news coverage of D.C. and Prince George's County has been well worth it. Among other things, it afforded me the opportunity to meet a lot of young black people who are fearlessly doing powerful things, like Sean Wilson, a twenty-year-old who is destined to be an elected official. That also includes people like Joshua Humbert, who founded Envest, a philanthropic nonprofit for African-Americans under age forty. I consider his work encouraging and a reminder of the abundant talent in our race – despite the negative imagery of blacks that's so often depicted in mainstream media.

While black folk have been "running things" in D.C. for years, Baltimore hasn't been in on the action for nearly as long. In fact, the city has had only four black mayors, the first of which was Clarence H. "Du" Burns, who was mayor for several months in nineteen eighty-seven after completing the term vacated by then-mayor William Donald Schaefer, who left to become Maryland's governor. Late that year, "Du" Burns was defeated for the position outright by former State's Attorney Kurt L. Schmoke, a Rhodes Scholar and graduate of Harvard Law School, who became the city's second black mayor when he was elected in nineteen eighty-seven. Schmoke served three, four-year terms, opting not to run for reelection in nineteen ninety-nine. Eight years later in two thousand seven, Shelia Dixon became the city's third black mayor, first female mayor and first black female mayor; however, she resigned in two thousand ten and was succeeded by Stephanie Rawlings-Blake, another black woman. Rawlings-Blake was elected in two thousand eleven.

But back to Schmoke. By being elected the first black mayor of Baltimore, he was able – just like Jackie Robinson and President Obama – to raise the bar on race relations and better position black people for a seat at the table.

When Schmoke left office in 1999, however, the O'Malley era began and things changed dramatically for blacks. Baltimore soon saw a financial shift, with dollars leaving the black community and going straight to the city's white business areas. In my reasoning, because the neighborhoods in East and West Baltimore didn't vote for O'Malley, opting instead to support the two black candidates who opposed him, those neighborhoods were terribly neglected during his tenure. That's what I believe, and I'm sticking to it.

I understand, though, and don't blame him in any way because that's just how politics works. To the victor go the spoils. In other words, he who is in power decides to whom the money goes. Naturally, once O'Malley took office, he wasn't going to reward dissidence. The Eastside voted for Carl Stokes, the Westside voted for Lawrence Bell and everybody else voted for O'Malley, including many black women. They thought he was cute but didn't realize he was also going to present a litany of obstacles for the black community down the road. Quite often, people tend to vote for attractive candidates without fully investigating their agenda.

O'Malley appealed to a lot of black people at the time because he had the pizzazz and charm to win. He ran a smarter, better-organized campaign, and further, the former administration admittedly didn't have a secession plan that would ensure passing the ball to another black mayor.

At that point, black political power in Baltimore began dwindling and so did the financial resources we once had. Adding to the problem was the fact that two black political giants in Maryland politics – Delegate Howard "Pete" Rawlings and Senator Clarence Blount, passed away. After a while, many in the black community felt like their community had been forsaken, and I sensed blacks were becoming less and less relevant to the city's operation.

O'Malley wasn't just a white man. He was the son-in-law of then-Maryland Attorney General Joe Curran. In the eyes of mainstream Baltimore, he was the crème de la crème of mayors. From the white community's perspective, O'Malley very well may have earned an "A" as mayor. But from my unapologetically black perspective, a view I know is shared by other grassroots folk, O'Malley gave Baltimore back to white people.

Of course, at the end of the day Baltimore is not just black or white. It's Latino. It's Greek. It's Ethiopian. I think the mark that was missed in the O'Malley administration was increasing pride in the city. Doing that was hard for O'Malley because he was not a native and lacked a certain connection to the indigenous peoples. Also, people knew he wanted to be governor and ultimately president and wouldn't be in Baltimore long.

So it was more like he was a 'temp' employee versus one committed to a long-term relationship with the people as did Mayor/Governor/Comptroller William Donald Schaefer. O'Malley's perceived as one who marches more to his own beat. And that's fine provided others are on that same page. When they aren't, however, that's the beginning of a major disconnect. When an office holder is going one way and his or her supporters are going another way, that's never good. Nonetheless, O'Malley has proven to be masterful at politics thus far and has an incredible tenacity. And, to his credit, he pushed the envelope on Minority Business Enterprise in Baltimore and across Maryland during his tenure; I am not sure, however, how many new black millionaires he helped create. I think his MBE advocacy, something of which he should be proud - seemingly began to taper off in his second term. In contrast with the Ehrlich days, many have told me that seemingly more black businesses benefitted with the Republican Governor.

Again, to O'Malley's credit, MBE was a critical issue he used to push heavily. Consequently, MBE became popular in Maryland. It brought critical light on the issue. That was and is always important. Now, whether or not this translates into new black millionaires – something I ask every politician who comes on my show – is a different story. This is why people like Arnold Jolivet, Robert Lee "Bob" Clay, Frank M. Conaway and Raymond V. Haysbert will be sorely missed. These men and others made sure black business opportunities were available. I cannot reiterate the significance of people like Pless Jones and his contractors association. Without people organizing black businesses to have a voice, to tell the elected officials what we need – then we will forever be cut-out of major state contracts worth billions of dollars.

A classic example is the MGM casino being built in Prince George's County. Worth a billion dollars, some African Americans are saying that this project does not have enough blacks getting part of the business. My point is that monitoring such issues is a constant task that has to be done. If not, blacks won't get anything. If you don't have a Bmorenews.com on the story, God forbid what happens next.

For me, the issue is always how a politician is going to be beneficial to African Americans. For me, the same thing you did to get the people is the same thing you gotta do to keep the people – no matter who you are: black or white; Democrat or Republican. Accountability is accountability and there are no two ways about it. You either served our interests or you neglected us: plain and simple.

Regardless of who is in charge, it is imperative that the black community have an agenda and it is important to stay true to that agenda. It is also important to prepare new leaders. I cannot otherwise blame anybody from outside of the community for anything wrong inside the community. That is an internal issue where, too often, we have had a continuum of the same old politics by the same group of politicians for far too long. Truth be told, some have maxed out and need to pass the torch to the next generation of leaders. The elders are needed for wisdom, but the ongoing struggle requires fresh soldiers ready and able to serve the people effectively and ensure that black people get a fair share of the pie, the resources, the money and everything in between.

Because as early as 2002, everybody knew O'Malley wanted to be president of the United States, his challenge was staying focused on the task at hand while simultaneously tempering his enthusiasm for higher office. He needed a solid body of work in Baltimore that would make voters want to vote for him down the road when he attempted to win office at the next level.

Everybody knew O'Malley was ambitious, becoming governor was next on his agenda and he wouldn't be around long. To his credit, he bowed out of the gubernatorial nomination process in 2002 to Kathleen Kennedy Townsend, who will go down in Maryland history as the first Democratic gubernatorial loser in decades. A member of the Kennedy clan, she just knew she had the election against the Robert Ehrlich/Michael Steele ticket wrapped up, but in the end she lost. Nonetheless, I give O'Malley credit for taking a backseat and allowing her to run.

Ehrlich won in 2002, largely in part because of Michael Steele, the brother who was his running mate and represented Prince George's County. They both ran on MBE as a targeted goal; they did an excellent job, too, ensuring that blacks got contracts. If O'Malley made MBE popular, Ehrlich took it to another level. People are *still* talking about those Ehrlich days when black businesses were doing the damn thing. Further, Steele's involvement in the election changed the dynamics of politics in Maryland, and to this day nobody talks of running statewide in Maryland without a black person on the ticket. Interestingly, and in some ways, sadly, it took Republicans to raise the bar in Maryland for black people. Maryland is a two-to-one Democratic state, and most of the black people in Maryland are Democrats, so one would think their own party would have best served them. Not the case. We've now come to realize the Republican Party can present the black community with bona fide options. But I say a little political competition is good for black people because it means our vote is less likely to be taken for granted. Notice, I didn't say it won't be taken for granted; I said it's less likely to be.

In any event, O'Malley challenged Ehrlich four years later in 2006, won overwhelmingly and served through 2014. In the

2010 election, Ehrlich didn't choose a black running mate but instead chose a blind white woman who was married to a Mormon break-dancer. His loss was colossal, as O'Malley took a page out of Ehrlich's book and brought on Anthony Brown, whose father is Jamaican and whose mother is Swiss.

From the Ehrlich Administration to the O'Malley Administration, one thing was clear: Prince George's County was commanding respect and they were not to be ignored. In Baltimore, however, there has been a void as elder after elder has died. There is a leadership vacuum that I hope is filled soon. Baltimore is nothing like it was for black people when I was a child. Today, Baltimore is slowly pushing black people elsewhere. Where Baltimore was once a powerful place for blacks, that energy which fueled the spirit of and commitment to leadership has seemingly shifted to Prince George's County.

And let me add, Prince George's has been good to me. The relationships I've built in Prince George's County have been well worth the effort because the folk in the county have far too much going on to be ignored. I've come to really appreciate a lot of the wonderful people I've met there, people who remind me of black progress and give other black people hope. Now granted, there isn't a state of euphoria in Prince George's County, as they have issues with public education and crime. But clearly they're doing a lot of things right in Prince George's County, and I'm extremely proud of that. I am also proud to know some of the players for indeed they are making history. For now, I remain optimistic that they can remain vigilant and push the envelope on black business and public education.

I can also say that just about every black person I've met at Woodmore Country Club, for instance, has a quintessential sixth sense for understanding that we, as a people, need to be better focused on our finances. Even more, many of the blacks I've met in Prince George's County are in some way entrepreneurial. From my vantage point, they have the attitude of a people determined to succeed, and I like that. I am attracted to that. It catches my eye.

To me, Prince Georgians have an "I can" attitude, which means losing isn't an option. There is an atmosphere of high expectation in PG County, which I love. At the end of the day, many of the businesspeople I've met and appreciate are determined entrepreneurs, like me, who are intent on making things happen.

Further, most every black Washingtonian I've met has had some semblance of political understanding, as well as an opinion on D.C. statehood. Their mantra, of course, is "No taxation without representation." (Incidentally, in November 2000, the D.C. Department of Motor Vehicles began issuing license plates bearing the words 'Taxation without representation'.) Just as most black Washingtonians who've crossed my path know their politics, virtually every black person I've met from D.C. has nothing but good things to say about the late Marion Barry. He's my absolute favorite black politician, and he was a joy to interview. Historically sound, he knew the political game like the back of his hand, and he loved black people beyond a shadow of a doubt. And the people know it. Hell, the man even took a bullet for the cause once.

Although re-gentrification has turned 'Chocolate City' so vanilla that the political reality of a non-black mayor is seemingly a matter of time, Barry's contribution will never be forgotten. I should add it was because of Marion Barry's government employment push that so many blacks were able to move to Prince George's County in the first place. He helped create an atmosphere for jobs and one conducive to blacks in business and helped many people, including former BET Owner Bob Johnson, who sold the network to Viacom for a reported three billion dollars.

Besides everything I just told you, the fact that President Obama and his beautiful family live in D.C. make it an even more attractive place for me to conduct business.

I thoroughly enjoy promoting businesses like Rollins and Associates Realtors in Owings Mills, or Realtor Angelo Cooper in the heart of Downtown Baltimore. And I get a rush out of covering the mayor, the governor and the first black president while producing an increasingly popular weekly news talk radio show, helping people find jobs, talking to prominent and poor people alike and interviewing them by way of videotape before sending the footage to the global media network my team has built. From time to time I even get to jump in a photo or two with some famous people, like Bootsy Collins. And sometimes I speak at the elementary school around the corner. Speaking to elementary school children is exhilarating because I know we must properly educate our youth to have a fighting chance in the struggle. Likewise, I know kids are eager to learn and haven't lived long enough to get jaded by society. And, if

I'm honest, it makes me seem larger than life. Now I know I'm not. But to little kids, many of whom, sadly, rarely travel beyond their neighborhoods or side of town, a brother who has traveled to Africa and the Middle East, to Canada and the Caribbean, who has attended events at the White House and who has schmoozed with some of the city's movers and shakers is nothing shy of amazing.

Despite the time I wasted here and there, I'm convinced I've produced a solid body of journalistic work. My accomplishments didn't come without struggle and disappointment, but the important thing is they came. I have twenty years of professional journalism experience under my belt, with a specialty in Maryland politics. Ultimately, I'd like to go national. I might not become a household name like Tom Joyner or Bill Maher, but I want to one day have my own syndicated show. I should note that during the completion of this book, I was blessed with my national television debut on TV One's "NewsOne Now" with Roland Martin. The guest host was Jeff Johnson. WPBRadio.com owner and strategic partner Frank Johnson, a man who loves media as much as I do, arranged that opportunity for me, and I'm eternally grateful.

In this, the Twenty-first Century, www.Bmorenews.com is more than a website and more than my pride and joy. It's a digital library that catalogs African-Americans, including the upwardly mobile entrepreneurs I encounter on a daily basis. It also features one of the largest African-American video news libraries in the world with ninety-nine percent original content. The other one percent typically comes from running a client's video. We have recorded over 2,200 youtube interviews in all.

When an article or video is loaded onto www.Bmornews.com, that person is then cataloged for life and their 'Google-ability' (the power to be picked up easily by search engines or search engine optimization) drastically increases with each new entry. So my clients have a vehicle that can boost their visibility on the net within a day or two.

This makes www.Bmorenews.com a virtual library with a specific target market of politically-savvy, upwardly mobile and often entrepreneurial African-Americans who have college degrees and own homes. We aim to provide the truth, as painful as it sometimes is. For better, preferably not for worse, our mission at www.Bmorenews.com is to inform, inspire and hopefully help improve the conditions of the African Diaspora.

Today, black folk have more resources than ever, but we don't always match that with common sense. We have six-figure incomes, advanced degrees, exorbitant houses and luxury automobiles like no generation before us, yet HBCUs, or historically black colleges and universities, are closing. I won't state an exact number of HBCUs countrywide because by the time this book is published, it may have changed. Suffice it to say there are slightly over one hundred in the U.S. now, a number that, sadly, used to be significantly higher.

American slaves, on the other hand, saved their nickels and pennies and quarters to build black colleges. They sacrificed so we could have a fighting chance, and in some instances we're making a mockery of their blood, sweat and tears. Hell, we're making a mockery of their lives.

I once did a radio show about a black college in Atlanta that was thirty million dollars in the hole in two thousand twelve. Don't tell me something isn't egregiously wrong with this picture. And, by the way, if black colleges and universities don't get with the program and start offering more online courses – increasingly popular and great ways to increase revenue – even more of them will be shutting their doors. I learned that last fact at The White House during an HBCU Summit on Entrepreneurship, a powerful gathering that featured former Bennett College President Dr. Julianne Malveaux and Dr. d.t. ogilvie of Rutgers.

Instead of making progress, blacks are steadily falling down the economic ladder. And let's be clear, in today's economy simply maintaining isn't good enough. While we're maintaining, others, particularly in the Latino community, are climbing the ladder. Thanks to the help of institutions with predatory lending histories, like Wells Fargo, for example, we now have an otherwise upwardly mobile black community that's befuddled and swimming in debt. This includes Greater Baltimore and Greater D.C., which were both hit hard in the mortgage lending crisis.

If you ask me, and even if you don't, some folk got in trouble with the mortgage lending fiasco because they were living above their means or closing on houses they flat out couldn't afford simply to try to keep up with the Joneses or to impress someone. Hopefully, people will wake up and smell the

Maxwell House and start discerning what's best for them and who they can trust.

Hopefully, more and more black people are getting serious about the future and desire, more than anything, to be a valid part of it. I'm tired of seeing the look of desperation on the faces of my people every single day. It eats me up now as it always has, so I make it a point to spread love as often as I can. When you understand how our people got to this state, it becomes all the more obvious that love is central to turning around Black America. I repeat: we need to listen to more love music.

Black people can fix our neighborhoods if preachers start preaching, elected officials start legislating, community leaders start leading and parents start parenting. Further, I really believe a goon squad is necessary to ensure the black agenda is at the forefront amidst 21st Century American politics. Yes! Our best and brightest, like my good friend Wes Moore, are needed at the collective bargaining table to help us form an agenda.

I'm reminded that Egypt was not built in a day. Therefore, issue by issue, one by one, we can reverse the madness in Black America. Small victories lead to bigger victories, small successes lead to more successes. Black Wall Streets didn't happen overnight. Folk worked hard. And they worked strategically and methodically.

To me, true empowerment starts with doing for self. Like Marcus Mosiah Garvey, Jr. suggested, we must take our destiny by the horns, and the true leaders will show us how.

Thus, www.Bmorenews.com is all about the empowerment of the community, about capturing the stories of those brave hearts who've decided to determine their own destinies by simply joining forces and working together to support black businesses and institutions. You know, we need to strengthen the institutions legitimately dedicated to black progress, and for me that doesn't necessarily mean the NAACP.

My good friend Marcus Murchison often reminds me of the NAACP Legal Defense Fund and the incredible work it has done from its onset. True dat. However, we need much more than that. I think a lot of times, even when the Congressional Black Caucus holds its annual legislative week in Washington, many people go for the parties. I need to hear a more vocal NAACP, one that has strong roots and history in Baltimore. I want to see an NAACP that mirrors the civil rights organization as it was during the days of Enolia P. McMillan, the first female president of the National NAACP, when black men and women comported themselves with dignity and respect.

We need institutions that are unapologetically committed to the plight of black people and that will unapologetically speak truth to power – as did King and Malcolm. Too often, our issues get lost in the sauce and are usurped by others, including feminists and "so-called" liberals. I'm unapologetically black when it comes to the issues. Further, I don't need a spokesman to speak on my behalf.

Truth be told, black people wouldn't need anybody to do anything for us if we had our heads on straight. Even though America is still hostile territory for blacks in many ways, that doesn't prevent blacks from spending increasingly more with black businesses and helping black institutions grow. Like Maggie Anderson and her husband showed us with the one-year Empowerment Experiment, in which they patronized black businesses only, if we use our heads we can come closer to living one hundred percent off black businesses. Heck. Many Latinos, Africans and Asians already practice this act of keeping their money in *their* communities.

It's no secret black folk spend a lot of money on Timberland boots, luxury vehicles, expensive rims and cell phones. You name it, and chances are good we give up a lot of dead presidents for it. And we shop when we know we shouldn't be shopping – like when the mortgage, rent or electric bills are due. We focus on the superficial and not what's real. Immediate gratification is a huge problem in the United States, and black folk got it bad. Oddly, I think this stems from a warped sense of entitlement. The truth is, we have everything we need to succeed, including good leadership. We just have to do a better job of grooming some new leaders who are addicted to common sense.

Chapter 10
Business Philosophy

I can honestly say it hasn't been easy to stay in business the past twelve years. And, given my propensity for politics, I'm well aware being on the losing side of an election can be devastating. However, it can be done – and with class.

Before I go on, let me first say being in business is an education all by itself and I certainly don't claim to be an expert on the topic. I'm just out here trying to make sense of things like everybody else.

I try to stay close to those who have successfully conducted business longer than me, to pick their brains and learn their secrets so I can apply them to my own business model. After all, what better way to grow a successful business than to learn from those who have done just that? Say what you want, but only a fool refuses to seek help from those who already are where he or she hopes to be. Now I may be a lot of things, but a fool is not one of them.

Running a small business requires incredible discipline, a lot of faith, and superhuman determination – especially in rough times. Successfully running this business is my goal – despite the plethora of challenges I face on a regular basis. Sometimes it's easy, but that comes only as the result of proper preparation, hard work and lot of integrity. Well, I guess if I'm going to keep it real, every now and then luck comes into play, too.

Entrepreneurship is not for everyone because entrepreneurs sacrifice like nobody on the planet. For instance, I vowed from the very beginning to invest proceeds back into my business, to be wise and not to fall for the chicanery of going shopping or spending unnecessarily every five minutes. That meant when a dollar came in, I had to reinvest it back into the business by paying the people who work for me and buying the necessary equipment, including computers and software, to keep the business going.

But I'm human. So that means every now and then a brother purchases a fly suit for his next trip to The White House or drops two Benjamin's on a meal at one of the finest and most upscale restaurants around. But for the most part, I spend less money on rewarding myself and more on growing my business because I've found the greater the sacrifice, the greater the reward. Likewise, you get out what you put in. That said, I aim to continuously upgrade my website and computer equipment. With the proliferation of social media, you have to keep your website in sync with the ever-changing technology. Along that vein, I'm a voracious reader. I want to know the latest news and be abreast of the most current trends – just like the big boys. New technology makes this doable, so I want the absolute latest in technology. And, of course, that requires money.

The point is, to have the latest in technology you have to put aside the money to pay for it. Not to reinvest in my business would be suicide. Consider this. When I first got in business, a new computer had everything on it. Nowadays, you must purchase the software a la carte, which, to me is a hustle.

Computers are like cars, and sometimes you need a mechanic. That's why I'm ever so grateful for Icetech.net and 1sqbox.com. William Hopson and Alexis Coates are the best computer people I know. For the past decade, they've bailed me out time and again. They're based in Baltimore, they understand my computer needs and they don't give me the runaround or any hassle when I need them. They are a blessing and a constant reminder that you're only as good as your team.

Ken Harris is known as a computer tech beast in PG County, and he has helped me out considerably. These people are a must if you run a computer-based business like I do. They keep me current, and I couldn't run my business without them. They are always in-the-know on the latest IT information, and that's the exact nature of my business: knowledge, information and timeliness. For me to be uninformed about current events or trends, or for my computer to be offline is out of the question. I simply can't have that! My computer gurus provide me with critical information that, when applied, consistently elevates my game.

Alexis, for example, suggested about six years ago that I start a Facebook, Twitter and LinkedIn page. Doing so was the last thing on my mind, but I quickly realized I had to get on board with social media to get to the next level. Long story short: it quadrupled our hits.

Clearly, not having necessary technology and equipment is like entering a football game without a helmet and pads, or like a politician waging a campaign without money. It's not advisable and won't get you very far. In my business, a broken computer can cost a candidate an election, result in an unsuccessful book launch or ruin an artist's debut. It can be the difference between a satisfied, smiling client and one who's stark-raving mad and ready to sue. Losing isn't an option for me, so I ensure I'm on top of the latest technology and that I pay my computer gurus what they're worth. When they're happy, my clients are happy. And when my clients are happy, I'm happy. It's that simple.

In a computer-based business, what can go wrong *will* go wrong. Therefore, I must have a continuous backup plan at all times. In my business, "what if" is very real, so I know I must be prepared for the unexpected, which includes Internet blackouts. Thankfully I've never experienced one, but I know of others around the country who have and, suffice it to say, it's not pleasant.

If you're an entrepreneur and think you've been blessed with the vision to birth a business, then maybe my story will inspire you or you'll be able to relate to it. Perhaps something will pierce your soul and give you a shot of hope. Ultimately, my prayer is this book will inspire people to dig deeper, read longer, write more and persevere until their goals are accomplished. At the end of the day, I know everybody has at least one purpose in life. The key is finding your purpose and becoming of service to others.

As I've stated repeatedly, this country hasn't been fair to people of color, particularly African-Americans. But I don't consider myself a victim. What I do think is black folk need to return to the basic values and wisdom of our elders. If we revert to teaching our children that they have to be three times as good as their counterparts, I believe we'll become successful once again. Of course, it won't happen overnight and will take a collective effort between parents, teachers, preachers, activists, journalists, politicians and promoters.

In all honesty, my biggest challenge is making people understand my services aren't free. I can't tell you how many times someone calls me up, asks me to perform a particular service – be it write a press release, help with a political campaign or what have you – and then balks at my help once I start talking about the bottom line. For the life of me I don't know why people think I work for free. If I'm not mistaken, and I know I'm not, slavery ended in 1865. And I don't mind telling you I'm not trying to reinstitute it. You may be laughing right now, but I kid you not when I say some people actually think I work for free. DMGlobal and www.Bmorenews.com are essentially a one-man shop, but many people with whom I've interacted sometimes mistakenly think otherwise.

Another challenge is finding good help. Still another is finding customers who can pay. So I constantly try to find ways to improve www.Bmorenews.com by sponging off the minds of successful business owners. I'm blessed to work with some pretty fascinating strategic partners who help me when I need them. Similarly, I'm there for them when they need me. Our regular business networking events are critical because they allow us to stay relevant, visible and to gather business owners, potential clients and potential strategic partners in one place for the sake of doing business and making new contacts. Building new relationships and maintaining old ones that are viable is critical in my world.

I was once told if you know five broke people, you will become number six. Thus, I make it a point to surround myself with people who are successfully navigating the business waters because I've found success breeds success and like-minded business people are a great source of inspiration. They understand the hustle. They understand the sacrifice. Some of these success stories are white, and many of them are black. In time, our goal is to expand the demographics to touch more White, Asian and Latino people because I think demographics will pretty much require that in years to come. But for now, we primarily concentrate on black folk.

I believe in presenting a quality product and like to give customers more than they expect. I believe business is a good thing, but repeat business is everything. I believe if you do right by people, they will do right by you by giving you their business and bringing more business to you from other business owners. Word-of-mouth advertising is quite possibly the best there is – and it's free. So, all business owners must be good at their craft and nice to their customers because without customers there is no business.

I'm not looking for special favors, but I do expect access. I've found not everyone is as loving as me, and I've developed a thick skin as a result. I've also learned it's critical to make solid business decisions.

Again, I'm no expert in the world of business. I do know, however, if we stay focused and keep God first, we can succeed in business and in anything else. There are countless variables, but I think the most important part of my business philosophy is simply doing what I say I'm going to do. One's integrity and one's word are everything. Over time I've learned my word is all I really have. So, I make it my business to do my best to bring honor – not shame – to my name. And that means doing right by people. No, it doesn't always go perfectly, but usually things work out in the end just as they should. So, like I tell my children: do not lie; do not steal; and let your work speak for you.

Chapter 11
Voice of the People – Developing the Baltimore-Prince George's Connection

The most specialized component to DMGlobal's services I've yet to discuss is very near and dear to my heart: the political consulting. This is the arena in which I tend to spend an inordinate amount of time during election season. I think it's of utmost importance that black folks have a powerful voice at the political table because we have greater needs than most other people in America. I want my people to have everything possible because we definitely need and deserve a better shot at a chance for a more prosperous life.

However, more often than not we're left out in the cold. And that's why I'm so interested in who's in charge. I need to know who those people are and what they're doing for my community. As a journalist, I enter doors through which most people dare not venture. Therefore, I know I have a special responsibility. And as a black journalist, I have the innate responsibility to always look out for my people. If I can be a voice – especially when it matters most, I will. Many times I help in print, and sometimes I help by making a phone call. Much of what I do is politically based.

Politics, the manner by which we determine who gets what, when and where, is part of who I am. If I can help my community, I will. And sometimes that may mean asking the question no one else will ask. My father always said a person has to beat their drum; and if that doesn't work, beat the drum harder. With that in mind, I aim not only to ask tough questions but to deliver the answers – or non-answers which is often the case – to our readers and listeners. The First Lady of the Black Press, Ethel Payne, had a similar reputation for asking questions. And so did the 101st Senator, Clarence Mitchell, Jr.

Beginning in Baltimore, and then extending to Prince George's County and Washington, D.C., covering the political developments in the black community is a mainstay at Bmorenews.com. This is our beat, and we aim to help make a difference. Although politics can seem very confusing, I submit to you we have to get better at the political game. Unless the black community gets on par with mainstream America in both major parties and as Independents, too, we will continually be shortchanged.

For instance, when I look at the Jewish community, I see they are a much stronger political force in American politics. I think black people can use their numbers to push most any legislation they desire. But it takes organization and the mass removal of emotion and ego to get things done.

Over the years, people have come to value Bmorenews' take on news stories, thus increasing our credibility. Beyond the DMV, people across the globe visit our website. Part of our task at Bmorenews is to be a watchdog for the community. I think people want to read our perspectives to contrast what the larger outlets are producing. And so, if we can add in a perspective that brings attention to the needs of Black America, we certainly will.

Because I've reported on so many politicians in twenty years, spent so much time with them and have been involved in some key campaigns, I've emerged as "grassroots spokesperson." It's said I have a bit of political influence, and I've established a reputation for telling it like it is.

Blacks comprise thirty percent of Maryland's population, so I bust my hind parts to ensure black folk have a voice, especially when it comes to politics.

I should mention that linking Baltimore, my hometown, with Prince George's County is important both politically and from a business standpoint. Since my first visit to Woodmore Country Club with fellow business owner and mentor William Hopson, I've been in love with PG County. I'll never forget that day I first went there because it was an absolutely beautiful site. 'Hop' took a picture of me standing by somebody's Bentley, which left an indelible impression in my mind. Interesting, the Bentley was green. And in case you didn't know, that color signals growth.

Since I attended a political fundraiser in Woodmore Country Club that featured Terry McCauliffe, a powerful Democratic operative at the time, I've made a whole new cadre of contacts – many that have been nothing but gold to me.

One of the things I love is that, generally speaking, a lot of the people in PG County 'get it'. They understand black folks have a hell of a better chance of survival in America if we stick together and work together. Those who truly get it also understand that those of us fortunate enough to graduate from college have an innate responsibility to return to our communities to help make them better. The visionary black folks in Maryland understand that Baltimore needs Prince George's and Prince George's needs Baltimore – if the thirty percent of black folk living in Maryland are to get their just due. Like my father often said, we have to help each other.

And so, connecting Baltimore and Prince George's has been a most important part of the growth of this business. We've strived to build viable relationships with a similar demographic, one that's majority African-American, like Baltimore City. At the same time, black Prince Georgians have a higher median income than blacks in Baltimore. Thus, covering Prince George's County is an absolute must for www.Bmorenews.com. It is imperative we have an ever-growing presence in this all-important part of the world.

Person by person, story by story, event by event, I began to connect with some really amazing people like Odessa Hopkins and Peggy Morris. I think because there are few media outlets in the county, let alone black news outlets, www.Bmorenews.com has been able to stand out in *Gorgeous Prince George's*. We've been able to provide some black news coverage and host several business outreach events there over the years, and I'm incredibly proud of that.

Twelve years later, we have a growing and viable presence in Prince George's County. More and more people know our name, and because we have a growing constituency there we've been able to learn the skinny about some of PG County's key issues, such as ensuring black contractors get a fair share of the construction projects. After all, it only makes sense.

Public education and minority business enterprise are two areas of critical importance to our constituents in PG County and Baltimore. And D.C. is no different. All three of those majority black communities have similar issues, so we began to ask similar questions to elected officials in all three jurisdictions. For example, we queried politicians about education and business with the knowledge that blacks in all three jurisdictions share similar sentiments and face similar challenges. In other words, we aimed to find the common thread, the common theme if you will, in all three locations. Another pertinent topic is ex-offenders. Given that Baltimore, PG County and D.C. are "chocolate cities" and there are many of us, unfortunately, imprisoned, that's a hot topic for those areas and for www.Bmorenews.com readers. There are simply too many black men, women and children involved with the prison system to be ignored.

So, considering my team is working with a smaller operating budget than the television stations and newspapers, we've learned to do more with less. We've learned to accentuate our strengths, in part by narrowing our scope and focusing on common themes and topics of interest to all three jurisdictions. Over time, I've realized the DMV is merely a microcosm of black America. We have wealthy blacks, and we have some of the poorest blacks in some of the worst socio-economic scenarios in America. We have tons of black professionals, and yet we have tons of black folks being adjudicated and under-employed. We have blacks in some of the top positions in the state, yet too many blacks occupy space at the bottom of society's totem pole. For instance, while Maryland is touted as having the best schools in the nation, the two worst school districts in Maryland are historically Baltimore City and Prince George's County. And while I'm proud of the black folk who live in PG County and are doing so well financially, I must say I'm disturbed at their academic status; they're at the bottom with Baltimore.

In short, this is how we grew beyond Baltimore. And this is also how being involved in elections became par for the course. I'm sure one might wonder how journalism and politics merge. Well, trust me when I say the answer is very carefully. Not only am I a journalist; I'm also a businessman.

Quite frankly, I like politicians who look out for black folks. And believe me when I tell you I know the difference between people who simply talk a good game and those people, like Marion Barry, who actually demonstrate their love for the people. As the saying goes, 'game knows game.' All ships tend to rise when you have someone like Marion Barry in charge. Say what you want, but the man mastered endearing himself to his constituents and, as a result, the people will never forget him. This is the kind of politician I like to see in office: a black politician who understands taking care of black people.

Having been under his tutelage on more than one occasion, I'll never forget the marching orders he shared with me. He encouraged me to continue educating people about the political process and about the power that we, as a community, have.

And that's exactly what I've aim to do: encourage those who follow www.Bmorenews.com to better understand the power of the black vote as well as the issues affecting us. Even more, it has become imperative to me that those issues also resonate with politicians. If the politicians aren't paying attention to our issues, then we at www.Bmorenews.com have failed. Not to pat myself on the back, but I know we've helped keep the black community's issues relevant. At least, that's what people tell me in the streets, on the weekly radio show and online. And hey, they can't all be wrong, can they?

To date, DMGlobal Marketing & Public Relations, the very proud Creator of www.bmorenews.com and the Black Wall Street SERIES *NYC *MD *DC *ATL, has been recognized each consecutive year in business:

*2014 Debut on national television, The Roland Martin Show, TV One, NewsOneNOW
*2014 Keynote Speaker, Head Start Baltimore Graduation, Morgan State University
*2014 Panelist, National Newspaper Publishers Association, Portland, OR
*2014 Community Leadership Award, VIPeVENTS Concierge
*2014 Lowes 4th Annual Basketball Tournament "Thank You" Award, Robert C. Marshall Recreation Center, Historic Pennsylvania Avenue
*2014 Social Media and the Urban Child Symposium Panelist, University of Baltimore

*2014 Black History Month Award, Land of Kush
*2014 Raymond V. Haysbert Entrepreneur Award by State of Maryland Black Chamber of Commerce
*2013 Mandela Award from Prince George's County
*2013 Omega Psi Phi Mu Mu Chapter Citizen of the Year
*2012 Baltimore Activist Award by Southern Christian Leadership Conference & The Solidarity Center
*2012 Renaissance Man Award by Sisters4Sisters Network, Inc.
*2012 Black Professional Men's "Rays of Hope" Awardee
*2011 Freedom Fighter Award by GCOMM Media
*2011 Juneteenth Museum's Legends Award
*2010 MomsRTheBest.com's Leadership Award
*2009 Voice of the People Award, CEO Business Café, Prince George's County
*2009 44th District Legend Award
*2008 Legacy of Freedom Award by the Paul Robeson Academy
*2008 Greater Baltimore Black Chamber of Commerce Citation
*2008 Engineers of the Year Awards Business Summit's "Men of Influence" Award
*2007 The Association of Black Media Workers (NABJ) 2006 Media Choice Award Winner: Best New Media, www.BMORENEWS.com's BTV
*Baltimore City Paper's 2006 Best Place to ... Get Political
*Baltimore City Paper's 2005 Best Enterprising Journalist
*2005 Distinguished Alumni, Coppin State University, Baltimore
*2004 Small Business Administration Business Advocate of the

Unapologetically Black | Doni Glover

Year Runner Up, Maryland

*2004 Distinguished Service Award, Black Professional Women

*2003 Faces to Watch, Baltimore Business Journal and countless citations from federal, state, and local officials.

With blood from my ancestors flowing warmly in my veins
I withstand the winds of hatred, and overcome the pains
Moving on and growing stronger in light of all these things
My dreams still relieve me, my heart forever sings

I am the pharaoh and the prophet, the greatest king of all
My queen, she stands beside me. Always we stand tall.
The Gold Coast is my homeland. Blessed is my place
For there isn't a single land that has never seen my face

I am black and I am beautiful, a child of almighty God
I have fought as a true soldier against each and every odd.
I am the son of the Madonna and the light of all the world
And my legacy remains for every boy and little girl.

I have flown the skies and sailed the seas,
and built the pyramids to a tee
I have taught medicine to those near and far
And have flown in spaceships to the stars

The hands of time can never erase
My ordained, anointed and sacred place
For God is with me all the way
I am unapologetically black and beautiful every day.

Conclusion

When I think back over my life, one word comes to my mind and spirit – "Grateful." I am so eternally grateful for the wonderful and glorious things the good Lord has done for me. I am grateful for my family, including the greatest God-brother in the world, Bishop Kevin Fernando Elliott of The Lord's Church in Baltimore's Park Heights Community; that church helped save my life when I was acting totally self-absorbed.

I am also grateful to have experienced some incredible places, like seeing where Harriet Tubman crossed the Niagara River at Freedom's Crossing in Lewiston, New York and like the Masai Village our team visited in Arusha, Tanzania. And there are other places I will never forget, like the Palestinian Refugee Camp I visited outside Amman, Jordan and the Ethiopian orphanage in Ambo Town – outside of Addis. I thank heaven for the chance to discuss world politics in Jordan in a kidnap zone with the late Arthur Murphy as US troops were landing to invade Iraq. And I will never, ever forget walking down the wrong street in the dark one late night in Tanzania or how jogging was so ubiquitous in Ethiopia.

Nor will I forget interviewing Pete O'Neal, the Black Panther in exile, or the US Ambassador to Jordan: such international interviews took my game to a whole other level. These and other experiences have broadened my scope and, prayerfully, increased my understanding of the world in which we live. From the hills of Jamaica to the United Nations,

I have been blessed better than most to see things many will never see.

I am most grateful for those opportunities to serve, like when we had a prison ministry over at City Jail for fourteen to seventeen year-olds charged with adult crimes. We called it the "Love for L Section" Ministry. When these young men have come up to me on the streets years later to say a word of thanks, nothing in the world can make me feel more worthy. Further, I greatly appreciate those humbling moments and life lessons that will never, ever be forgotten. These may have taught me the most about what not to do and how not to treat people. Karma is indeed real, so treat people the way you want to be treated.

It should also be noted that trials and tribulations have indeed come. I made a heap of bad decisions. And I learned that there are consequences for our actions that may take years to settle. However, no matter how many mistakes we have made, we can decide right here, right now that enough is enough. I am proof that change can indeed occur. You just gotta want it with every fiber in your soul for God looks at our hearts. I've learned that the mind is a very powerful tool and if we tap into its strength, we can do more than we might imagine. As long as our heart is pure, the infinite light in the universe will find its way in – some way, somehow. I also know that when one door is closed, another is bound to open. All we have to do is just hang in there.

Today, I am a much better man. I do my best to keep it simple and be of service to humanity. I think I'm learning to be more mindful of others. Personally, I prefer to keep my circle tight and to surround myself with good, unconditional people who've got my back. That and faith is all I need.

As for the state of black people, I am 100% convinced that we have the ability and the power to change our course. I believe that the keys to success are education, finances, and voting; these are our tools. Education by any and all means is a must. Mastering our one trillion dollars in annual spending is another. And voting responsibly and holding elected officials accountable is the third. When the masses of black folks find the treasure in our history and master these three tools, collective success is inevitable. As for white supremacy, I think it has terribly disaffected blacks *and* whites. I think the energy some place on dominating others could be better spent on finding more humanistic solutions to the challenges we face in the broader human race.

Beyond all of that, I think the black community must look inwards for the solutions and the answers. Personally, I think we are losing sight of our deep, rich history and the good ol' values our ancestors instilled in us. We must return to the basics of love, friendship and mutual support. On the other hand, being stingy, entitled and ungrateful sure are no help to the cause of black empowerment. Even more, our black bureaucrats cannot forget that they have an innate responsibility to look out for other blacks. Truth is, the solution is in helping each other succeed – whether we like each other or not. The Jews do it. The Koreans do it. The Latinos do it. They are known in the US for working together. Blacks must return to such basics because they *do* work. Blacks have to begin to make education paramount again, as did our ancestors. I am one who believes just about everyone should go to college or technical school. I think everybody needs skills in an ever-globalizing society as ours. So, I'm not for a lot of excuses; I think a solid education is essential for the black community and America overall. Fiscally, we have to make the black dollar circulate seven times before it leaves our hands. It's real simple. This means that we do not have to like each other; however, we must indeed spend money with each other. This is where love is so important; if a person's business is hiring ex-offender, for instance, they definitely deserve the community's support.

We have to resurrect our love for the black man and the black woman. This will necessitate a lot of forgiving, but it can indeed be done. As we forgive and begin to correct our ill behavior, we will then have a chance. I am clear that nobody is going to save black folks except black folks. No president or governor or senator or mayor can do what the people can. This is America, and its track record of service to African Americans is delinquent. I have very little faith that the government is going to go out of its way to correct the ills of the past, like slavery, like the bombing and burning of Black Wall Street in Tulsa, like the Tuskegee Experiment, like hundreds and hundreds of lynchings of men, women and children. Nope! I do not have much faith in reparations.

Instead, I choose to look at what we can do to chart our own collective destiny in the land our fathers built.

The journalism, in retrospect, has always been in my soul. I have written since the age of 6 with intense pride from my first love letter to my 6th grade report on "Roots" by Alex Haley. I have also been afforded television opportunities since childhood when I first appeared on WJZ TV 13's "Bob Turk and the Sunshine Kids" and "Evening Magazine" with Baltimore Oriole third baseman Brooks Robinson and other James Mosher All-Stars. So, becoming a journalist is not surprising. Being an entrepreneur has always been in me, too. Today, I delve in both realms heavily with a distinct penchant for politics; even more, I am crystal clear that the politics is supposed to translate into either business or jobs that benefit my community. And when that does not happen, we have a problem. And problems require solutions. And that is exactly where I want to be: in the solution.

Politics captures my essence because it is the process of dividing up the resources, and from my unapologetically black perspective, somebody representing black interests needs to be at that table – whether it is in City Hall, the State House, the White House or at the United Nations. And – as my dad advised me in court one youthful day, that person at the table has to be able to "speak up!" That representative, on behalf of the 40 million or so black people across America, cannot be afraid to *speak up* on our behalf – in the same spirit of other great people of the darker hue who, too, faced incredible odds and even death. Harriet, Frederick and Thurgood quickly come to mind. Malcolm and Martin, too. They were not afraid. They instead spoke truth to power, worked for freedom and justice, sacrificed for us, and ultimately made life better for black folks and the rest of the country.

For me, it is essential to understand the interrelationship of politics and economics from a black perspective so as to help other black people better understand the game. We have to keep our eye on the money and stop believing a lot of the lies that politicians utter. Quite frankly, I'm not convinced a lot of black elected officials can count. If we can count, then we should be getting more than the crumbs that are dropped for us to eat while other communities feast daily. It makes absolutely no sense to me to continue to put my precious political capital in the hands of people who are not delivering a solid return on our collective investment.

Further, I've found that this Black Political Economy is applicable to East Baltimore, Kingston, Pretoria – wherever black folks are. In short, my interest is in seeing our labor and our resources better serve us as opposed to serving everybody *but* black folks.

I pray, too, that I have that leader-spirit of serving the people; I pray it is deeply engraved in my soul such that I can effectively do my part and help make things better for my people. Whether the issue is redistricting, the number of black businesses on the latest casino construction project or the City of Baltimore snatching people's homes for exorbitant water bills – I know that I have a duty to help make life better for the other people in the community. And, of course, this means grooming future leaders for approaching elections.

To my young people: Do not give up on your dreams, regardless of the circumstances. I have seen too many people overcome otherwise impossible odds to accomplish their goal. So can you! Take education seriously, use your manners, and do the work; all of the work. By the way, obtain a passport and then go and see the world; your perspective is bound to expand. Remember, there are no shortcuts to success. You have to put in the time and do the necessary work in order to reap the full rewards and fruits of your efforts.

Do take your education seriously. People around the world would love to be in your shoes. So, bust your butt doing your work, and then do some extra work. Hard work typically pays off. The trick is finding your passion. Once you identify your passion, it will lead you to your purpose. When you find your purpose and fulfill it as only you can, you will find peace. I say, take some time to get to know yourself. The rewards are priceless.

Also, we all make mistakes. They happen, but they do not have to mean the end of the world. The key is to learn the lesson at hand. When we don't, life has a funny way of making us repeat the class.

Unfortunately, we live in a world that is angry with our blackness. It isn't my fault we come from greatness. It isn't my fault we're beautiful. It isn't my fault that black people have contributed so much to help improve this world - from ancient times to today. I say: Celebrate blackness!

You define you, not another. Not the television; not the web; not all of the misguided writers of history. So, walk in your destiny with your head held high because you have absolutely nothing to be ashamed of and everything of which to be proud: kinky hair, straight hair; no hair, curly hair; from the lightest of skin to the darkest of hues: Muslim, Christian, or Hebrew. It just doesn't matter because it's *all* beautiful. There is no way on God's green earth I will ever be ashamed of my blackness for I *am* unapologetically black.

Finally, when it is all said and done, be absolutely sure to give the good Lord above all of the praise and all of the glory. I have found that if you keep God first in all you do, you can do anything except fail. So, *do* give God His props.

This is my story, and I pray you are a tad more informed, inspired, and empowered to go out and accomplish your dreams, goals, and aspirations – no matter how big or small. Remember, with a closed hand, nothing gets in and nothing gets out. However, with an open hand, there are endless possibilities. The moral to the story is to help somebody.

Afterword - "Doni and Me"

As I remember, it was the fall of 1991 when I first encountered one Mr. Donald Glover, son of a prominent Baltimore funeral director and mortician and a student in the new Media Arts Program at what was then-Coppin State College in Baltimore Maryland. Little did I know that the meeting during fall registration would forever alter my life and many of my notions about the city itself.

I was a middle aged college professor at an HBCU, and as such, I was feeling an acute sense of awareness about such schools and what their very existence could mean to present day and future black students seeking a degree in the ever growing field of media communications.

After reading "Megatrends" by John Naisbitt, which is a groundbreaking piece of speculative literature about the coming revolution in the communications world and its propose impact on all our lives, I had set out to help carve a niche in that relatively new field for young African American students studying in college then and in the foreseeable future to make a place where our students could take advantage of massive opportunities that were soon to present themselves in American life.

The book was and still is considered the ultimate but, speculative authority on where our society was headed in this communication revolution which was just emerging in the 80s and 90s.

Now it must appear that I have abandoned the story of "Doni

and Me," but I assure you dear readers that I have not. For it was at this locus that Doni and I first met.

Young Mr. Glover, hardly out of his 20's, and finally ready to make a serious commitment toward finishing his college education, enrolled at Coppin State and as luck would have it settled on this new major: media arts. It was the very same program written by a few of us Coppin professors that was approved as a part of the Degree Granting curriculum at the college.

As it turned out, Doni who is a very impressionable young man, at least in terms of new and exciting ideas, found himself in my "Introduction to Mass Communications" class. The history of our journey together begins there in that class!

My first order of business in that basic introductory course was to introduce students to the groundbreaking works of John Naisbitt of "Megatrends" fame. By now the book, which was about 3 years into publication, was enjoying widespread success across the globe. I felt that it was important to have students look seriously at the business and technical trends that would hold sway on their future careers. They needed to know about all the emerging opportunities and how to capitalize on them for themselves.

While there was a regular text to the course, to be sure, the students and I spent a great deal of time pouring over all this new and valuable, first-time information. I wanted each of them to be steeped in the knowledge of how to use this information in their media careers, stateside or abroad.

From the very first day, Doni seemed intrigued with the Naisbitt message. That message was...come live this future.

But, I digress. So, from the moment I began explaining the Naisbitt philosophy, I could see an intense interest develop in Doni as he literally absorbed every word about both of the books "MEGATRENDS" and "MEGATRENDS 2000". So very intense was his interest that we sometimes spent many long moments after classes, (he had me for three classes in one semester) discussing the meaning and scope of each of the two books.

I am firmly convinced that it was his interest in this man's version of the future landscape of mass communications that has fueled Doni's passion for the field. To the point that it is sure to have birthed the iconic "Bmore News" and now all of its other publishing offspring, as well!

Even then, I could easily trace his motives. So, when years later, after I had moved on to teach at Morgan State University, I learned from Doni that he planned to follow a career in publishing a new kind of news "organ" for public and community consumption, I was not surprised. I say "organ" because to me "Bmore News" as it's known draws from many areas and is all about the new media realities spoken of in "Megatrends".

In many ways Doni Glover is a force in the establishment as well as the promulgation of the new media opportunities that we discussed often in the early '90s. I will say this. I don't think that I had a clue at the time that Doni would go on to be the giant he has become in the industry and in the Baltimore community.

Oh, he had the talent for sure. I think I was fixated on getting the message out to my students and did not fully grasp that it could or would affect one of them: Doni Glover.

As I recall, the history of the Media Arts Program at Coppin State University in the early to mid-90s was interesting; I am always reminded of the many colleagues who helped to establish the program, the many contemporaries like Marconi Combs who aided and abetted the programs' growth, the faculty in the English Department, and the students like one Mr. Doni Glover who took a vision, adopted that vision, adapted that very same vision ... and then worked that vision like no other!

I am indebted to them all ... and I am most to Doni. He is truly ... the son I never had!

Professor Ronn Nichols

CPSIA information can be obtained at www.ICGtesting.com
Printed in the USA
BVOW02s2242290415

397821BV00001B/2/P

9 780692 404386